ZELDA'S SECRETS

Ramona Harper Ferguson

KISMET Publishers Ltd

Many stories include my memories, from my perspective and I have tried to represent events as faithfully as possible. For privacy reasons some names, location, and dates may have been changed. Some characters, and incidents portrayed in this book are fictitious. No identification with actual persons (living or deceased), places, buildings, and products are intended or should be inferred.

Book Cover by KISMET Publishers

Illustrations by Adam Ferguson

Edited by Denver Murphy

First edition 2024 Second printing June

Printed in the United States of America

Published by KISMET Publishers LTD

kismetpublishers.com

ISBN – 978-1-7393870-5-1

To the Love of my Life, Adam Ferguson

I have only been able to start and finish this book with you in my life encouraging me. Thank you for supporting my vision. Your brilliant and creative mind is only matched by your good heart and compassion for people.

To Hiram, who is like a son to me

Thank you for always cheering me on. Your tenacity and courage give me hope. Your kindness and compassion for others is evident in everything you do. You are a beacon of light in the dark.

To Engin Akyürek, famous Turkish actor/author

Your writing motivated me to write short stories. The story of Fatmagul gave me the courage to write the first story. As actor/author you bring joy and depth into our lives. As a human being you have a magical force that inspires us.

To the women who have cheered me on

Jackie, Bobbie, Jacki Lynn, Lynne, Pammie, Tina, Janine, Mira, Larisa

I thank you and love you so much for your belief in me.

To my brother Michael Cherry,

for loving me unconditionally

And to my mom Inez Jackson

for always allowing me to be me.

ABOUT THE AUTHOR

Ramona Harper Ferguson grew up in Montclair, NJ. She has been writing on and off all her of life, but this is her first published book.

Ancestry – Descended from the ancient Maasai people in Africa and the Vikings.

Interesting Fact – Her great grandfathers both fought in the Civil War, one as a Union officer the other as a Confederate. And they had neighboring farms in Virginia.

Preface

It occurred to me that no matter how deeply things are buried, my subconscious dances in the tandem with my conscious mind to reveal certain beliefs that I hold dearly and fiercely spring forth and surprise me in my writing.

One of the most profound and most difficult to embrace is my belief in the phrase "People need love the most when they deserve it the least", So I confess upfront, that in writing this first story neither I nor the character were able to honor this sentiment.

CONTENTS

Publishers Note 133

INTRODUCTION

I arrived in Montclair, NJ only months old. I remember lying in my crib alone on the 3rd floor of my Aunt Florence King's Victorian house on Forest Street amusing myself with the noises I discovered could make. I loved that house. It had 7 bedrooms but the tiniest bathroom on the second floor. Two steps in either direction and you were at the sink, commode and claw foot bathtub with no shower. The house had a back stairwell where I used to hide. It went from the kitchen to the upstairs used by the servants to the former owners. Aunt Florence and Uncle Archie worked there as maid and butler before they bought the home in the 1940's. My favorite parts included the 6 fireplaces including one in the kitchen that got replaced by a potbelly coal burning stove. I also loved the bookshelf in the second-floor hallway and would spend hours at age 3 copying what I saw, meticulously in pencil in the blank pages at the front of those books.

The former owners had left a croquet set in the basement, and we entertained ourselves in the hot summer months with badminton and croquet in the yard. We sat on the back stoop in silence excitedly waiting for the first lightning bugs to appear, quenching our thirst with frosty glasses with fresh squeezed lemonade. My favorite things about the backyard, other than the pink roses, were the cherry, apple, and pear trees, and the grape vines next to the garden. Every spring I eagerly helped my aunt plant string beans, tomatoes, cucumbers, peppers and lettuce first as a child, then as an adult.

But the sweetest treat came from the cherry tree. I was reminded of this in the most unlikely place, reading a short story by a famous Turkish actor Engin Akyürek entitled, what else? "The Cherry Tree". I went on to publish his book of short stories Sessizlik (Silence) in English because among other reasons, he inspired me to write my own short stories. It was both serendipitous and kismet my finding Engin Akyürek.

Adam, my well-read husband, said after the first story it's painful but powerful. Keep going! After the tenth story he declared Zelda's Secrets a bestseller.

My my how well the Universe works! Call it what you want, God, Creator, Allah, Buddha. Life is both magical and marvelous if you have faith and are patient.

I am proof that you are never too old to set a goal.

Be Careful What You Wish For

***

If I wasn't so bold, so self-assured and borderline cocky, would I have suffered so badly?

I was always good at getting whatever I wanted before I ever knew the word "manifest" existed and meant. Before it ever became a buzz word.

As the wildly fun and decadent '80s drew to a close, I decided to get serious and stop getting high. Nearly everyone I knew got high. They simply couldn't refuse the allure of a *"white line babee."* It was our pop culture, part of the excess of the times, a status symbol. You've seen the *Wall Street* films with Michael Douglas and Leonardo. My hubby and I were no exception, we worked hard, made lots of money and happily threw it away on expensive dinners, trendy clubs and white powdered weekends with friends. But for me it was time to stop partying and going out all the time, and very importantly time to stop working for other people. I decided to go after what I wanted and what I wanted was my own modeling agency.

So, I did it.

I have always loved the high fashion glamor and excitement that belonged to the magical realm of Elite Models, Ford Models, Wilhelmina and other top NYC agencies, but my agency was mostly models who were those "slice of life" "girl next door" types. The pretty girl advertising the first hair scunci. The attractive mom selling the miracle mop. Real stories, relatable vignettes with good looking people selling things. Like the Meryl Streep vs Charlize Theron or Jennifer Hudson vs Beyoncé type. Like Meryl and Jennifer, I'm also that girl and I feel compelled to share a bit of my personal slice of life, girl next door, story. Of course,, if it were up to my ex, Dennis, I may or may not have been able to share this with you. As I looked around my office filled with stacks of unopened envelopes containing headshots and comp cards of people dying to be models and actors, I thought to myself Dennis would have hated all of this.

I glanced over my copy of the morning Breakdowns, a term for the list of roles and casting calls that were faxed over each morning to tell us what Hollywood and NY were looking for in film, TV, commercials etc. It was definitely nothing he would want to be a part of, but all that mattered was I loved it. There was never a mundane moment in our offices. Yesterday Julia Roberts' brother was looking for a mature woman to play nude in a scene opposite him, and tomorrow my child talent was going to meet with Rob Reiner in a final audition for a role in his movie. Nope, there was absolutely nothing he would like in this world I belonged to now.

Thinking back to my teens and early 20s, I wasn't really a model, but I modeled. I was pretty and had great, bouncy, white-girl hair when chemically straightened, so I did hair ads and learned how to work a runway from the best walking coach of the day. Michael Harris taught us girls about using an invisible head-string to achieve great posture, how to strut down that catwalk leading with the pelvic bones and how to twirl! None of us were as good as he was but I could stop on a dime spin like a ballerina, hands on waist, arms at 45 degree angles and step out of it with grace and attitude. There were six of us girls under his tutelage and we pranced, posed and practiced giving one another attitude through glares and head tosses for hours. But in spite of a great runway walk at 5'8" I needed at least an inch more, so I dropped from my usual

128–132, down to 116 lbs. My waist shrunk to just under 24". I didn't choose to diet; I just made the decision that thinner would look taller. Back then I didn't understand the power of speaking and thinking something into existence. I figured I was just good at achieving whatever I wanted. In fact, the reality was I just wasn't that self-aware. I did whatever I felt; I acted on impulse guided by only my own inner logic and compass.

My grandmother would tell me, "Girl, everything that pops in your head flies right out of yo mouth. You best be careful what you wish for, you just might get it." My grandmother had many stories and beliefs that, as a child, sounded ominous and frightened me. I would sleepwalk often into her bedroom and, one night after thinking the chair next to her bed was the toilet, I confided in her that I was also having weird dreams and recurring nightmares. In one dream something was lying on me, holding me down and I was paralyzed – unable to move my body or speak. I tried so hard to scream out terrified for help but nothing would come out. Perhaps that's why I fear that Edvard Munch painting so much, it reminds me of myself. My Grandma said that dream was a spirit trying to tell me something from the other world. I thought, *oh hale to the no!* I didn't know and didn't wanna know nothin' about "spirits", so naturally I found no comfort in her words in addition to no comfort in sleep.

In fact, it terrified me so much I hated falling asleep. As I got older, I generally dismissed her words as folklore but perhaps she had both the wisdom and just enough superstition to recognize my power, and in her way tried to warn me to be more aware.

***

"Good models are merely clothes hangers," Oscar said.

Oscar was the designer I modeled for, and he said that to me, to all of us actually, so I just wanted to be the best clothes hanger possible. I practiced diligently and did my best with the inches I had. As a result, I opened shows and I had my moments in the spotlight, and even signed a few autographs for adoring fans. One day, as we were finishing a show and chatting about our aspirations, Diana who was 5'11" and a flawless clothes hanger with hauntingly beautiful hazel eyes and honey caramel colored skin, said to me:

"You really shouldn't aspire to be a model."

"Why not?"

"I see you more as the owner of the agency. The businessperson behind the desk."

I felt crestfallen but I laughed. At twenty I really didn't know what I wanted to be, but in that moment I just wanted to be the best model, and her words affirmed what deep down I already knew. I couldn't be a High Fashion well-paid model. I would never go to Europe and walk for Yves St Laurent, or shoot a Vogue magazine cover. I was a "pretty girl next door" type. I was a "slice of life" kind of girl. At that moment I wasn't too pleased. That didn't sit well with me and my I-can-do-anything competitive spirit. The realization that it was out of reach wasn't a pleasant feeling at all.

I realized that once again I was too accustomed to thinking about and getting what I wanted. I often thought about why other people suffered because they weren't as lucky as I was, and about how I could help them. I simply didn't understand then why people didn't just decide what they wanted and claim it for themselves. For example, take my high school best friend, Darlene. I knew she desperately wanted to dance because she talked about it and the Alvin Ailey Dance company in NYC all the time. I thought she was so beautiful and would make an amazing dancer. She was a willowy 5'10" and had the long, graceful arms, legs, neck and sleek hair of a dancer, so why not? One day after school I decided to surprise her. I was on such a high all that day, I could hardly contain my excitement or keep my secret. I had called and gotten the address and took her from Jersey straight to the Alvin Ailey Dance location. So, imagine my shock at her reaction. In disbelief I started yelling:

"What? No! You're joking! But why????? Why not??!!!???"

The words were jumbled and tumbled out of my mouth in both disbelief and disappointment. We went back and forth before she ended it by saying:

"Because I don't want to and I'm not going to."

She refused to even go inside and get a brochure! It took me years to even begin to understand why. It took decades to understand that the pain carried in the souls and psyche of broken little boys and girls is a tragic, horrible weight, and that the healing requires attention and awareness, intention and time. That fear is the enemy of love and passion for what you really want to do in life.

***

"Each day through my window I watch (him) as (he) passes by. I say to myself you're such a lucky (girl) to have a (guy) like him is truly a dream come true." - Just My Imagination by The Temptations reimagined

Over and over, I sang my version of this song for hours and hours after I saw this hot guy and decided I was definitely going to make him mine. Who cared that as captain of the basketball team he only dated cheerleaders. *Not I*, said the fly sitting on the wall, watching. Who cares that I was already dating one of his teammates. Not me, besides that had run its course after a few months anyway. We both knew it would come to an end after his senior prom and we just hung in there until then. In fact, I didn't even take him to my prom which was two weeks later, I went with a college senior I'd dated on and off. In fact, that was a mistake and, looking back, I realized I didn't even take a photo to carry the memory. But I dated a lot of guys in my teens and I had three boyfriends and now had my eye on the next one. I was secretly glad I was voted Biggest Flirt and the girl most likely to give you blue balls. Older boys had been frightening me by shoving unwanted, unwelcome hands down my pants since I was six but now I could control whose hands I allowed, and just how far around the bases I'd go. No one was getting a home run until I was good and ready. Besides, I fulfilled my deepest need for true love and meaningful connections with books. When I graduated 6th grade my award for being Best Reader was a blue and beige paperback copy of Jane Eyre. I loved it. That little book introduced me to the world of Jane Austen, and Charlotte and Emily Bronte, and I willingly and happily plunged into their world of lonely love-starved women who worshiped the men they couldn't have initially. I wanted the love in those stories, a love that was so passionate it would set me on fire. I wanted a man that worshiped me. I wanted to be his sunrise and sunset and the greatest love story ever told. I wasn't the girl to swoon over movie stars and put their posters on my bedroom walls. I wanted the real thing. Someone who would die for my love. Oh, I knew it was over the top and dramatic, but I didn't care. I wanted it.

The hot guy's name was Dennis, but everyone called him by his nickname. I can't write it here because then everyone would know who he was. I concocted a plan of action with Darlene and Chrissie and drove over to his town to visit my friend, Connie. I strutted to the park, with my crew in tow in freshly ironed tight jeans and a pink halter top, to watch him and his friends playing basketball. That day I couldn't take my eyes off him. I drank him in, all 6'7" of him, and he was perfection. His hair looked so soft and formed tiny wet curls at the neck. His nose showed some Native American heritage and the beautiful mocha color of his skin glowed with sweat. His hands were so graceful I imagined them sliding down my body. I wanted him to wrap those long arms around me as I tilted my head back and got on tippy-toes as he bent towards me for a kiss. I imagined those perfectly shaped lips and dreamy eyes coming towards me. I watched intently, my eyes narrowed to mesmerized slits. He laughed a lot, tossing his head back his Adam's Apple bobbing up and down. I thought about what I knew about him. Everybody, and I mean everyone, loved him. Girls wanted him. Guys admired him. He was well known in the state as an incredible player but who had genuine humility. He was confident but not cocky. Quiet and self-assured, he had an ease about him that was in the way he walked and talked. Everyone talked about what a nice guy he was. I never heard even one half-bad thing about him. Finally, I turned to my girlfriend Connie and said,

"Okay. He's mine."

"I heard he has a girlfriend. You know, Althea Smith light skinned light eyes good hair?"

"Hhhmmm."

So I said nothing to him even though he glanced my way. I just watched. When I got home, I went straight to the family room, put on that song and laid back on the sofa thinking about him. Every day for hours I sang that song and wished he were mine. Exactly four days later the phone rang.

"Hi, can I speak to Zelda?"

"This is Zelda, who's this?"

"This is Dennis, well you may know me as _____"

Oh my god! Oh my god! Did I squeal, squeak or scream before clasping my hand over my mouth??! Praying I did none of the above while kicking my feet in the air I heard:

"Hello? hello?"

"How did you get my number?"

"A friend. I saw you at the basketball park that day last week."

"Yes I saw you too."

"Do you want to go to the Sly concert this weekend?"

"Don't you have a girlfriend?"

"No."

Shocked and speechless I slowly hung up the phone and just stared at it. Jumping straight up, I stubbed my toe on the coffee table, barely catching myself as I pitched forward slamming my shin.

"Damn it! All I need is a bruise! Damn it that hurts!"

Shocked back into reality I grabbed the phone and called my girlfriend.

"Connie!!! Oh my god Connie, you will not believe what happened!!!"

I spent the rest of the day calling every girlfriend and discussing every single little detail. I'm certain I got on everyone's nerves but maybe not since they were all excited for me.

He drove a big car that made me feel slightly insecure and in awe. I looked at his hands and those long fingers holding the steering wheel. The seat was all the way back to accommodate his long legs and boney knees. He leaned back, molded into the seat, as if part of the leather. He had put a white towel on my side and, as I sat on it, I wondered what was underneath it. Stains? Holes? Where had that towel been and what had it been used for? I had decided to have him pick me up at my mom's house and I thought about my mom and grandmother looking up at him when he walked in the kitchen to meet them. My mom pulled me to the side, and smiling said what a nice guy he was.

"He's so polite."

"I told you so Mom, he is the nicest guy. Everyone loves him."

That night at the concert we ran into his ex – Althea – and I was so jealous! She actually tried to flirt with him in front of me. It was ridiculous! What right did I have to tell her to stay away from him on my first date, and start a ruckus right down at the front of the stage? He, however, just laughed that easy-going laugh of his and wrapped his arms around me and kissed the top of my head, saying"

"Calm down, Bunny."

I was his and he was mine. We had talked on the phone every day for hours since his first call. We had connected so fast we couldn't believe it ourselves. We were madly in love.

The next weekend I went to his mom's for dinner and to meet his aunts and friends. I adored his mom and aunt, who became great friends with my mom.

Dennis had a waterbed. I hated it. I was also afraid about what it meant to be in his room, lying across his bed. Rocking. I had imagined it so many times, but this was real. He was holding my face and kissing me, just like in the movies and romance novels I loved. He was so gentle as his hands moved over my shoulder and down the curve of my back, as if memorizing each bone and muscle he touched. I relaxed as he whispered in my ear, "Are you okay?" Nodding my head, I was lost in his eyes when his lips touched mine. How he got my mouth open and gently started sucking on my tongue I'll never know, but I melted literally in a pool of wetness and desire, with the water moving beneath me as the weight of his body bore into mine. He whispered *I love you* as he entered me and I opened up, welcoming the heat that filled me up and took me on a magical journey.

"I love you," I whispered back.

We were inseparable after that night. We only had July and August and part of September before he would have to leave for college. We spent most weekends at his house so he could practice. Sometimes I went to the courts, other times I helped his mom or went shopping with her. In the evenings we would play poker with the family before shutting ourselves in his room. He was everything I wanted in a guy. Tall, handsome, kind hearted, funny and attentive. He worshiped the ground I walked on, as did I in return. He showered me with affection and attention. Just the way he looked at me made me shiver with joy. He would shake when I would touch him and fold me into his arms and shower me with kisses, murmuring how much he needed me. I drowned in it. It was a drug and an addiction. It was intoxicating. He was my Heathcliff, my knight in shining armor, and I was elevated to beautiful in his love that summer. We were beautiful together. In his arms I felt safe. I could fall asleep, unafraid of the dark with him. Unafraid of the nightmares of dark twisted grotesque monsters reaching out their long arms to me. Before I was constantly falling into a deep abyss, and I would wake with a start just before I hit bottom. I dreamt endlessly about being chased and unable to escape, but finally I was safe falling asleep in his loving arms.

I was attending school locally, so as the time drew near for him to leave for college, we decided I would travel to visit him on Thanksgiving weekend, and we would just count the hours until then. After he left, life for me fell into a routine of work, school, friends and his weekly phone calls. He was on a basketball scholarship, so his practice and game schedule also kept him very busy.

***

CHAPTER 2

Five black guys and one white guy lived in a house that was formerly inhabited by nuns. The black guys had all been recruited from out of state to play basketball. That's what I found when I arrived in the northern tip of Washington State. The house, a nondescript white structure, was in a desolate area surrounded by nothing but fields of half burned patches of brown grass as far as I could see. I imagined it would have been a perfect location for nuns but for me it was a scene out of a dreaded horror movie. The sort of place you might find on a Haunted Horrors tour. The sort of place that needed a good sageing, if that was a thing back then. A mile or so down the road was a gas station, a small food store and, way off on its own, a solitary phone booth sat at the intersection of two roads. Every day it drizzled or rained. I was not at ease there. It didn't speak to my spirit, plus I wasn't excited to be with five male strangers. But I was so happy and excited to see Dennis and so it was easy to pretend that everything was wonderful. The guys in the house were nice enough but I wasn't accustomed to so much testosterone, so much “locker room talk”. I didn’t grow up with it so I tried to be okay with it, but I also wasn’t accustomed to Dennis being around just guys in that environment either. During dinner one day, when they started talking about girls whose pussies smelled like tuna, I was over it. Call me whatever, it was too vulgar for me. Still the five days flew by by in a blur of sweet love and hot sex, so when Dennis got on his knees, wrapped his arms around me and begged me to stay, how could I refuse him one more week?

One night we decided to do something different and go out to a restaurant. I sort of expected the stares since there were no people of color in the area before these ballplayers arrived, but I wasn’t prepared for people asking if they could touch me because they had only seen black women on TV. I admit I was shocked. I grew up in a very diverse upscale town and this was like something out of an old novel or black and white movie. It was the ‘70s and I proudly rocked my massive Angela Davis Afro and people came up and asked if they could touch my hair. That was okay, I guess, but I would never think to ask someone white or any color to touch them or their hair. A perfect stranger. I was flabbergasted, then stupefied when I was asked:

“When you bleed, is your blood black or red?”

“What did you say??”

“When you bleed, is your blood black or red?”

“Are you kidding me?”

Surely this woman was joking. But no, she was not. As my aunt would say, “Dis tew much!” I didn’t realize it at the time because I’m not a worrier nor easily intimidated but my uneasiness grew.

I couldn't identify it, but I didn't feel completely safe and I felt no inclination to school an entire population of people who saw me as an oddity. Another time and season perhaps, but at eighteen that was not part of my story. I had now been there almost two weeks and so, when Dennis begged me to stay through Christmas, we argued. Reluctantly I agreed again.

One night in this former nuns' home of strangers a fight broke out. It was silly and it started with an argument over playing this one song *Me and Mrs Jones* too many times. Whenever these guys drank MD2020, known as Mad Dog, I got nervous because that alcohol truly lived up to its name and made them 100% loco. That night they were so out of control I stayed in my room. I was stunned when it turned racial and I heard the threat of bringing in the John Birch Society which was headquartered nearby, and as Andersen Cooper says was "the QAnon of its day". Then I heard the sound of glass shattering, screams, shouts and the thumping of bodies being hit and falling. Terrified, I curled up and pulled the covers over my head. Why am I here? I should be in school. I have a job. I should be with family and friends, not in a house with six men, five of whom are strangers. Besides, I didn't know anyone there. I certainly didn't trust anyone other than Dennis, and he seemed a little different. I had nowhere to go and nothing to do that didn't involve him or a basketball game. I did meet the coach's wife who talked to me and gave me her number, but she was older, with two small children, so we had nothing really in common. All of this was going through my head again when I approached Dennis the next day.

"Dennis, we need to talk. You know I love you and want to be with you, but I want to go home. To my family, school, work. I need to go home."

"You promised me you would stay through winter break."

"No.... I said Christmas and I want to book a flight for the day after."

"But you can't leave me alone on New Year's Eve."

"Dennis, be reasonable. It'll be over a month. I will lose my job. I've already lost part of this semester. Plus it's not fair to me."

"You don't love me anymore. The way you used to."

"WHAT???? Why would you say something so ridiculous! Of course I love you."

"Is there someone else you want to go back to?"

"What?! Dennis! Are you crazy? Quit being ridiculous!"

Back and forth, round and round we went with him pleading and me trying to reason.

"Let's just talk about this later," I said, finally exhausted and getting angry at the way he was looking at me filled with suspicion.

The next day we had the same conversation, and the next day. After the third day when he returned from school my mind was made up. I was no longer happy being there, in fact I was unhappy. I was not a person to remain in a situation that made me unhappy. I had always made my own choices. I decided what I wanted and didn't want. I didn't understand it then but looking back now my carefree spirit was suffocating in that house, in the energy of that town, around so many people with whom I had little in common. All day I sat with nothing else to do but wait for him to come home or go to a game to watch him play. I had no books, not even magazines. There was no car and no neighbors. There was no phone and it cost $2.43 a minute to make a phone call home, so I couldn't spend my days chatting if there was a phone in the house. Besides, I didn't want anyone at home to suspect things weren't perfect. I didn't want them to worry. One day I went to school with him thinking I'd find joy in my favorite place, the library, but so many people came up to me asking the same things: can they touch me, touch my hair etc. so I left. My brain that craved the excitement of multiple projects was getting no stimulation, no oxygen. My entire world was revolving around him. There was no *me*. I wasn't the beautiful girl starring in her beautiful love story anymore. This was not even my slice of life story anymore.

"Well, you can't go."

"Dennis, I've made up my mind. I'm going."

"You will NOT leave me until I say so." And with those words he pulled me up and into his arms.

I looked up at the face of this guy I loved so deeply and felt a teeny tiny prick of something unfamiliar. For the first time our lovemaking was not so tender, and I was not such a willing participant at first. But he had a way of making me want him and so I connected to his need in the slight tremble in his fingers, as they touched my pelvic bones and slid up my sides to my breasts. I felt the quiver in his belly as his flesh met mine, and his heavy breathing and calling out my name when he came was enough for me in that moment.

The next day I waited until he left for class. I pulled on my precious Calvin Klein coat I had worked so hard to afford and my

6” red and blue platforms since I did not bring sensible shoes on this micro trip and left for the mile or so trek to the phone booth. In my hand my fingers clutched the piece of paper with Nancy the coach’s wife’s number on it.

“Hello Nancy? This is Zelda, ______’s girlfriend. I need your help Nancy.” Suddenly silent tears flowed and my voice shook uncontrollably as I explained to her what was happening. She agreed to make flight arrangements for the following week and would come to pick me up.

“Do you need me to come now, Zelda?”

“No, I'm fine, I can hang in there a few more days. Besides I don’t want _______ to know.”

“Okay, bye.” Hanging up I heaved a sigh of relief.

He snuck up on me.

“You don’t want me to know what??? What are you hiding from me???!! Who was that? What’s his name??”

Turning around I barely got the word “nothing” out when he punched me so hard that within the confines of that small space my head slammed against the side of the glass before I crumpled to the ground like a bag of rags. I felt the next blow as his shoe connected with my cheek. I saw the sleeve of my Calvin coat was bloody and muddy. Could it be cleaned? He kicked me again. He stomped me in the head and kept kicking, I think. I don’t really know how many times. Did I scream? I don’t know. I blacked out or passed out. It’s all a big blank in my mind.

I woke up alone in the bed in his room. I lay there, slowly starting to remember what happened and I momentarily froze with fear.

Moving in slow motion I put my hand to my face and gasped, it was then I realized I was seeing out of only one eye. Did I lose an eye? How long was I lying there? Where was he? Glancing around and determining I was alone I got up, moving like an 89 year old, and went to the mirror. I didn't know the battered, swollen, bruised, cut, discolored image looking back at me. One side of my face looked like the Elephant Man, it was so distended. My lips looked as if the pink insides were outside. How could they possibly be that big? My tooth was chipped. How long did I stand there staring at the horror looking back at me? I have no idea. I just stood frozen, listening to the sound of my own breathing. Was I in pain? I don't remember if I was or wasn't. How could he do this? Why, why, why? Why would he do this? I know he loves me so how could he do this? What do I do now? What will happen when he returns to the room?

I heard the click of the latch of the door. He stepped inside and time stood still. He stared at me and slowly fell to his knees sobbing and wrapping his arms around me so tightly I couldn't breathe. I was silent.

"I'm sorry, I'm sorry, I'm sorry Bunny."

How many times did he say that?

Trembling hands, whispered *I love yous,* pushing me back on the bed.

"No," I said but it didn't sound like my voice. It sounded so far away.

"No,no,no,no,no." It hurt to even breathe.

His full weight was on me, smothering the me that was not me. I was dry as he rammed into me. Did I scream or whimper? His hand was over my mouth, so I must have screamed. The bed was moving and rocking and my head was slamming against the headboard but I wasn't there.

I was busy thinking about things and creating other stories in my mind. This wasn't happening to me. The romantic hero of the story never attacked his heroine. Only the bad guys and monsters harmed the heroine. The knight in shining armor would never hurt a hair on the head of his princess. Nothing bad happened to the slice-of-life girl-next-door, or did it? This wasn't me, this wasn't my story. The next few days were like a movie playing over and over that always ends with the girl's head slamming rhythmically into the headboard while the person she was not just lay there, humiliated and afraid. She did as she was told because she saw in his eyes the danger if she didn't. She couldn't go to any of the other male strangers for help and so she hid in the room when they were home and counted the days until she would leave.

***

"Zelda? Zelda?" I heard Nancy's voice. I heard her knocking on the door.

I flung the door open, and we looked at one another.

"Come. Grab your wallet and purse. Don't even pack. You're coming with me. Hurry."

On the plane ride back to the east coast I looked in my makeup mirror and touched up the bruises as best I could and put back on the sunglasses Nancy gave me. My brain hurt from the effort but as hard as I tried, I still couldn't understand what and why it happened. We were so in love. It was such a pure, sweet, innocent kind of love. We were one. He was everything I wished for. He adored and worshiped me. He needed me to breathe. Ours was the greatest love of all time. He was such a sweet, kind and gentle guy. No one would believe me. I didn't believe it.

So, who was this monster? How did he come to be my monster? How could I be in love with him? Engin Akyurek, my favorite actor, today says* that there is a monster that exists in all of us and, in the face of a traumatic event, it's all about how you handle the monster, or it will take over you.

*those words were translated from Turkish so that is what I thought he said, if not my apologies to Engin.

***

CHAPTER 3

I didn't recognize the girl who landed back at Newark Airport, but I watched over her because she didn't know what she was doing. She took two buses and shuffled the five blocks home from the last bus stop. Her aunt had an eight bedroom house and she'd rented a room there for the past year. Thankfully when she arrived no one was there to ask questions. Suddenly she was beyond exhausted and the stairs to the second floor seemed to go on forever. Going to her room she could do nothing except drop her purse and pull out her pajamas. She ran a steaming hot bath, poured in Epsom salts and laid back in the clawfoot tub, and surveyed the physical damage, thankful that nothing was broken. Her bruises were various shades of purple, blue, red and yellow. It wasn't that serious, she thought looking in the mirror after her soak. The face is looking better and in a few days should be nearly normal. It's not that serious, she reassured herself. No one died. Heaving a heavy sigh she dressed, went in the room, slid under the covers and fell asleep.

The loud ring of the phone on the side of the bed jolted her awake and reflex made her grab it.

"Hello?"

"Zelda? Bunny?"

Shaking, she hung up on him. Seconds later it rang again. She looked at it for a long time and let it ring. What was there to discuss? She just wanted to go back to her normal life of work, school and out with friends, and put what she had witnessed out of mind.

"Please don't hang up, Bunny. I have to see you"

Phones back then didn't have a way to shut them off or even unplug them from the wall. It would just ring non stop unless you took the receiver off the hook. After a while it would make a loud annoying noise that could be heard in the next room to remind you it was off the hook. She tried everything possible not to hear it. Not to go crazy.

"What do you want, Dennis? Please stop calling me."

"Please listen to me, I love you."

She hung up, wrapped the phone in a blanket and stuffed it in the closet, praying the ringing would stop. An hour later she took the phone off the hook and wrapped it up again. When she couldn't bear the muffled sound anymore, she put it back on the hook and wearily climbed back in bed. She couldn't bear one more long exhausting sleepless night. But as soon as it was on the hook. Ringggggggggggggggggggggg

Days later she awakened one morning to the realization that the phone didn't ring all night. Breathing in deeply, thanking God for that tiny bit of peace and knowing she had a busy day ahead, she took a quick shower, got dressed, and shouting goodbye to her aunt, sailed out the door. The hairs immediately stood up on the nape of her neck and arms, and the sour taste of fear rose in her mouth as acid churned in the pit of her stomach. Dennis was standing at the curb leaning on his car. Then walking towards her, then moving faster. Her hands shook so badly she could barely get the key in the door and escape inside. She raced upstairs to her room, slamming the door shut.

Ding-dong, ding-dong, ding-dong, ding, ding, ding...

The doorbell rang and rang. Her aunt knocked on her door.

"Zelly!!! Zelly, what in the world is going on?? Who is ringing that bell like that??!!"

"Auntie don't answer it! It's Dennis!!"

"Why is he ringing ma bell like that?? Sides, ain't he at school??"

Ding-dong, ding-dong, ding-dong, ding, ding, ding...

"I don't know! He was supposed to be at school"

Ding-dong, ding-dong, ding-dong, ding, ding, ding...

"Dis tew much!" Housecoat billowing behind her, my aunt rushed downstairs to the door.

"Dennis stop ringing this bell! She don wanna see you right now! Stop!"

"Auntie, can you tell her I want to talk to her? Can you open the door?"

"Boy, did you hear me? No, I'm not opening no door wit you actin a fool! Now go on home until she wants to talk. And don be ringing ma bell like that no mo! Like you crazy!"

Listening to them, Zelly felt a knot in her stomach as her mind raced, thinking about how all those recurring nightmares of being chased – her hands shaking trying to unlock a door, unable to escape – had come true.

She pulled herself together and got her aunt to drive her to work. I was grateful she did not have classes that night. When she returned home the phone rang all night. Each time she put it back on the hook, unable to take that loud, jarring noise as it rang. Even though it was muffled in the closet she could hear it.

The next day she looked out the window and he was there again. She left out the back door and her aunt again drove her to work. She focused on her work as best she could. She fell asleep sitting in the stall on the toilet until her friend came looking for her. After work it was also a school day, and she arrived early and went to the library.

"Bunny."

Her blood ran cold. Her head whipped around at the sound of his voice. She paused for a second before jumping up and racing out the room, down the empty halls not knowing where to go. She saw someone go into the ladies' room and ran in behind her slamming the door to the stall and locking it.

"What are you doing in the ladies' bathroom?" someone yelled.

"Bunny." She looked up and his eyes were looking over the stall at her.

"Bunny, please, I need to talk to you. I can't let you go. I need you."

Two sets of women's voices screaming now.

"Get out, get out, get out!!! Oh my god, I can't believe you're doing this to me!!!"

Zelda was shrieking at the top of her lungs.

What happened next? She can't remember what happened next.

After whatever happened on campus Zelda made the decision to go to her mom's and stay for a few days. She no longer felt safe at home. So, she sought sanctuary at her mom's with her other siblings and grandmother. She told her mom Dennis was pestering her, but she didn't tell her the whole story. She scarcely had one day of peace when the doorbell rang.

"Mom, if that's _______ I'm not here. Please don't tell him I'm here."

When she heard his voice at the door she wished she had told her mom everything that was going on because all hell broke loose. Shouting back and forth between him and her mom. Dennis rushed down the hallway to the kitchen where she was. Her eighty-year-old grandmother was knocked down by him. Her twelve-year-old brother tried to hit him from behind with a bat. He punched him and she saw blood splatter on the wall of the hall that was too narrow for so many people. Screams from other family members. Threats from him of what he would do. Someone called the cops. Everyone was outside screaming. Dennis took off like a bat out of hell, his tires adding to the screams. Up until that moment her home had been a safe-haven and a wonderful, peaceful environment. Her mom, though strict, never spanked them, no one hardly ever raised their voices, no one definitely ever cursed. She had brought this monster into their peaceful home. This foul-mouthed maniac who busted her brother's lip and knocked her grandmother to the floor. She was shaking with the gravity of what she had done, and afraid unknowing what the next day would bring.

The police arrived in the aftermath and said: "We will file a report but there's nothing we can do unless he does something physical to your daughter."

"Are you kidding me??? He threatened to kill my daughter!!!"

I'd never seen my mom like that. Well on one other occasion.

"Zelly, I'm calling Brenda right now and she'd better get her son under control, or I will!! He's not going to threaten you like that. Don't you worry about him. I'm going to deal with this myself."

They spoke and Zelda never asked about the conversation, but it worked. After a few days of peace and quiet she breathed easier and went back to her aunt's house.

***

The next day, walking out the front door for the first time, she felt a moment of panic but after looking up and down the street she relaxed and walked to the bus stop. It was a work and school day, and parking was so inconvenient that the bus and the walk to school was simpler. It was only five blocks to the bus stop and by the time she was halfway there she was feeling better. She was counting steps when the sound of tires squealing and brakes slamming made her swing her head in that direction, but before she could look in disbelief, he was out the car and, with a vice-like grip on her arm, pulling her in after him, across the big bench seat. Slamming the door, he pulled off. Thoughts raced through her head. If she jumped out and ran, he would catch her before she got to safety. It would be better to agree to anything he said and so she listened to his rambling words and told him she loved him, and she would be his girlfriend again. But he didn't believe her and became increasingly more agitated. He accused her of sleeping around and wanting someone else. It was all nonsense of course but when she said that it only made him worse. Breathing heavy, panting out of control like a wounded animal, he told her he couldn't live without her and if he couldn't have her no one would have her. That seared through her brain and she tried another tactic.

"What movie do you think that we're starring in???? Listen to yourself!!! Let me out and I will forget this ever happened. You can go on with your life and me with mine. You're not like this! You're not this person Dennis!"

"You made me like this! You did it! You, you, you!!!!"

Was it possible to speak with this level of ferocity and velocity? She felt like covering her ears to shut out the madness – to escape the fear of this nightmare.

Suddenly she had a clear and heightened sense of awareness. They were pulling into a park, and everything happened in seconds, but it seemed in slow motion. In a split second she absorbed several things.

She knew she would not leave that park alive with him.

She saw a police car parked by the building for restrooms. It was about half a football field away. She saw the car was empty. She did not think whether she could outrun a 6'7" star basketball player that distance.

The car was still moving when she flung the door open and ran. She could hear him screaming her name. She heard his Converses stomping the leaves in the grass. The sound of his breathing moved closer and closer, but she didn't look back. She just ran and ran, and she focused on her target, the police car.

Surely guardian angels must have carried her or given her wings because she outran legs twice as long and fast as hers, leaped into the back seat and locked the doors.

He roared her name over and over, demanding that she get out of the car. She screamed over and over for him to leave her alone.

She saw the officer running out the door at all the commotion.

"What's going on here??"

"He's going to kill me!!!!"

"What's going on here, young man?"

"Officer, I'm sorry, my girlfriend didn't take her medicine today."

"What? What?!!!!! He's lying!!"

She screamed and sobbed hysterically.

He yelled. Back and forth they went.

"Step out the car please, miss."

"No, no, no, no! I can't! He's lying!! He knocked down my grandmother and punched my brother. We called the police..."

She knew she sounded hysterical and out of control while he was calm but she also knew she would not survive the day if she couldn't convince him.

"Young man, why don't you just leave and you can straighten this out with her later?"

"I'm not going no-fucking-where without her."

I could not believe my ears. The officer did not address him but spoke into his walkie talkie.

"Ahh, I'm going to need backup at this location..."

Then to Dennis:

"Unless you want to go to jail, I suggest you go elsewhere and leave her alone. I will take her home."

***

Chapter 4

"If you love somebody
If you love someone
Set them free." –sung by Sting

He traveled two towns away, but the police officer drove me to my mother's house. He was a white officer in a predominately white town, and we must have looked like two out of control teens. So much could have gone wrong in that situation that day but thankfully he was caring and compassionate. He even listened while I tried to explain to him this beautiful love story that became a nightmare.

I didn't yet understand or have the words myself, so I just rambled on. I still don't and so I filed it away in my box of things to be examined later. I do wish I'd gotten his name to thank him later, because he surely saved my life.

The reality is some people suffer because of what they wish for, and others suffer by being afraid to wish. Some wish for the wrong things and others think they are asking for what they want, but they're not.

As for me, dear reader, I still boldly write my wishes in the sky amongst the stars and when they bring me too close to the sun and burn me, I hang them on the star and move onto the next.

Oh, and yes, my grandmother was right all along about this, as well as many other things she told me. *Be careful what you wish for, you just might get it.* I have learned to be much more aware and intentional with my powers.

As for Dennis, I never saw or heard from him again after that day in the park.

Until last week.

Last week, forty years later, he posted on my Facebook page:

Reasons to be Cheerful

"If you are a dreamer, come in,
If you are a dreamer, a wisher, a liar,
A hoper, a pray-er, a magic-bean-buyer...
If you're a pretender, come sit by my fire
For we have some flax golden tales to spin.
Come in!
Come in!"
– Shel Silverstein

***

"Stop telling stories, Zelly!"

My grandmother's words echoed in my head . This time her words brought a smile to my face because I was born to tell stories. Although I knew "stories" in her dictionary meant lies. So what? Lies? Stories? It was so hard to get to the Truth. And there are levels to lying.

"Girls grow up and marry their dads"

So said Marla, my friend, the therapist. Was that the truth?

If so,

Who does a fatherless girl grow up to marry?

I really didn't want to hear any psychobabble or theories on women seeking father figures. It's true I didn't grow up with my dad in the house. So I drew a life sized cardboard cut out, that I kept in my closet of the man I wanted to be my dad. I often wondered what my real dad would have done that day I was followed, or when Dennis stalked me.

OK so I made up the cardboard cut out part. Or is it a bold faced lie? See what I mean? Lies have levels. I didn't even have a picture in my bedroom, let alone a life sized phantom dad. Certainly I have pondered over the years what impact having no father in my life had on me. In fact, I asked Chrissie the other day, my bestie from childhood, whether or not I complained about not having a dad and she replied.

"You never talked about it. You didn't mention it."

Perhaps I should consult a professional like Marla since I don't recall that I've ever said to anyone, not even myself, "I miss not having been a daddy's little girl." Didn't everyone wish for a mom *and* a dad? What was wrong with me? Or was I lying to myself?

Had I heard about and internalized too many stories about girls who had been molested by male relatives or women that had issues around their fathers to worry about a dad?

Oh I had moments as a child when I'd visit Chrissie's house with her mom, dad, 2 kids and 2 dogs that went on amazing vacations together. On those occasions I thought it would be nice to have a dad but I didn't really want one that bad.

My mom on the other hand and her 19 siblings grew up on a Virginia farm blessed with the same parents all under one roof. My mom, a quiet reserved person with a quick nervous laugh, had the distinction of being the baby girl. She wasn't big on sharing her past. I can count on one hand the tales she told me of growing up. In fact I can count them on two fingers.

Once she was chased by a big dog who, when she fell in her panic to outrun him, he raced right past her. That dog was hell bent on his own mission and that mission didn't include one of the Jefferson girls. The other story centered around the fact that she was not allowed to date nor wear stockings until she was 21. One of those stories was a lie and who knows perhaps they both were lies. Never can tell with her.

I never even heard my mom mention her dad, and I always presumed that he passed away when she was a toddler. So I was very surprised, shocked in fact to find out when she was in her 80's, that he died when she was 19. Even then she referred to him by his full name Johnny Jefferson not dad, certainly not daddy. She also always addressed her mom by the more formal salutation of Mother.

What did my mom's silence about these things tell me? What does anyone's silence tell you? Nothing good. The road to truth is not silence.

I, on the other hand, have lots to say about my childhood. It was mostly a happy cheery blur of good memories. Well there was that problem with older boys when I was six, but that was just an inconsequential blip in the big scheme of things to come. Doesn't it always seem that when things are going too well something inevitably happens? A sneak up and bash you over the head killjoy. Some of it I suppose is just to keep you on your toes and humble and grateful. It can be something big or small, like when your bills are all caught up and the car breaks down. Although that doesn't count since that's a sign you ain't doing somethin right. You need to make a change. Some things seem to happen for no damn good reason. Is it kismet? Are they all life lessons? Well then as Oprah once said and I paraphrase, *Lawd I don need no mo lessons today.*

***

I had just turned eleven and was obsessed with the song *Summertime* from Porgy and Bess. "Oh, your daddy's rich and your mamma's good lookin', so hush little baby don you cry..." I belted it out, throwing my arms out to the side, head thrown back. What a wonderful life, 6th grade graduation was coming and I was on top of the world! I went shopping with my mom and bought the prettiest dress in the store. It was yellow and white with a white lace crinoline underneath and a yellow ribbon around the waist. I had matching yellow ankle socks with pretty white lace trim and my grandma polished my black patent leather shoes with Vaseline until they shone like new.

"Now they look like new money," she said, beaming at her handiwork.

I was grateful to her for the little things she did like ironing my clothes every Saturday for the week. It bothered me that she thought I was too outspoken. I thought it was good to have a voice. After all, I was truthful, mostly. My favorite uncle called me "the lil lawyer" because I had a winning argument for everything. If only I could talk my grandmother out of making me wear a starched cotton full slip stuffed into my pants and saddle shoes! That slip was the bane of my existence. It bunched up around my middle and looked like I was wearing a cloth diaper, 2 or 3 diapers in fact. But I lost that argument every day.

I was excited about the graduation ceremony and especially the awards to be given out, and I was not disappointed. I was a little embarrassed for getting so many awards when others got nothing. When it was over, I strolled out the auditorium holding my bounty of books in my boney, little arms. I had received the Best Artist Award and a scholarship to the Art school at the museum.

Two years before I heard on the CBS news that the Red Cross needed volunteers. I passed by the Red Cross building every day walking from school down Park St. so the next day I went up the massive stone steps and knocked on the enormous red wood door to offer my help. A tall thin blonde woman peered down at me over black rimmed cat eyed glasses. Her eyes registered surprise but she greeted me warmly and walked me down a hallway into a room. There sat several middle aged white ladies around a large conference table making cards. She introduced me as someone who wanted to volunteer and they smiled and welcomed me and I happily joined them. By age 10, I had learned how to answer the switchboard when the operator took her break. My mother was only too aware of my independent nature and so it was no surprise when she agreed to let me walk to my art classes on Saturday mornings by myself.

I was so excited and happy about my upcoming classes I talked non stop at breakfast that morning. It was only a twenty-minute walk but I left at 8am for my 9am class. I was feeling exceptionally cheerful, walking and skipping along in my brand-new white bobby socks and Keds, singing "these boots are made for walkin..." I pulled out of my pocket my remaining two candy cigarettes and took a puff before crunching down on them. Oh, the small pleasure of tasty chalk and powdered sugar melting on my tongue.

I was the youngest in the class and a little bit intimidated by what we were asked to accomplish over the next few weeks. I wasn't used to that feeling, still it was a challenge that I welcomed, or did I?

***

The third Saturday that I had art class I was followed. White male 52 years old, dark hair, 5'9". My stomach is in knots just writing about it all these years later. That Saturday I was sauntering down the street humming and lost in thought, pretty much like Prissy in *Gone with the Wind*, when I heard a man's voice say:

"Little girl, would you like a ride?"

She ignored the voice, afraid to even glance sideways. Her steps changed from lackadaisical to brisk as her short stick legs and white Keds moved as quickly as they could. He continued to keep pace alongside her.

"Would you like a ride? Come on, I can take you home." The sly attempt at sweetness in his tone made her feel sick and creepy.

A group of people emerged from a house at that moment, and she took the opportunity to dart down an alley that would put her on busy Bloomfield Avenue. Shaking, she marched down the street as fast as she could, breaking into a run down the final block. She ran in the house and raced up the stairs to her room and flung herself on the bed. She didn't know what to think or do. She only knew if she told anyone she wouldn't be allowed to go back to art school. She pulled the covers over head and listened to her pounding in her ears that was her own heartbeat.

The third time he followed her, she had decided to go to her aunt's house after class which was about a thirty-minute walk in a different neighborhood. She felt the car before she saw it out of the corner of her eye. It was that same big car, a white Lincoln Continental.

"Hi, would you like a ride today?"

She shook her head vigorously from side to side barely getting out the word

"No."

"Come on, you can get in."

She decided to glance over to see who he was. She wished she hadn't done that. He leaned down in the car, crooked teeth bared, smiling sweetly except his eyes and beckoned her to come.

She was a few steps from the Walnut Street Candy Store and she ran the distance, sprinting into the store past the front counter.

"Hey lil Zelly! where you goin so fast?" nobody said from behind the counter.

"Nowhere!" she shot back, quickly moving down an aisle pretending she had found something very interesting on the shelves and trying to make herself invisible. Her heart was pounding in her ears so loudly she thought it impossible that no one heard it. Suddenly, she felt something long and hard pressed against her back. She heard heavy breathing. She bolted down the aisle and raced out the store at full speed, and fled around the corner the block to her aunt's house. Why did scenes from my worst nightmares always seem to come to reality? She didn't look back like I did in the nightmares. She heard heavy breathing but still she didn't look back. She raced around the back of the house and burst through the screen door into the kitchen.

"What on earth? Chile, what happened? What's wrong?"

The realization he had touched her caused a feeling of terror and sheer panic to overcome hee. Shaking she burst into tears. Sobbing uncontrollably now that she felt safe, she told her aunt everything. She pleaded with her aunt not to tell her mom. She did not want to give up her reward. She did not want to give up her art classes.

BITTI*

We walked up the stone steps of the police station and my mom clutched my hand in hers. I couldn't remember when my mom last held my hand, if ever.

"Where do I go to report a crime?" She asked the man behind the desk. I heard the sound of her heels clicking on the marble floor and it sounded incredibly loud echoing off the walls. I heard the squeaking of my freshly polished sneakers. I hated when they made that sound. The white polish my grandmother put on them was too much and they felt stiff and uncomfortable.

Finally seated across the desk of the officer, my mom said to him:

"I'd like to report a man who followed and molested my daughter."

The policeman shifted his gaze to me.

"Why don't you tell me what happened? Take your time and start at the beginning. How old are you?"

"My name is Zelda Taliaferro and I'm eleven years old."

I talked and talked and talked some more. At some point he pulled papers and files from a drawer and looked at them. I stopped and he beckoned me to continue. When I ran out of words he said:

"Ms. Jefferson, we know this man. We have had many complaints about him. He has molested several children but we cannot get anyone to file a complaint and follow through with going to court. They just don't want to put their child through it."

My mom looked down at me for a moment before saying:

"We will do it. We will take him to court. No one is going to ever do that to my daughter and get away with it. He needs to be put under the jail!"

"If you cannot afford a lawyer, we can appoint one to your case. We will start today with her written statement."

"Thank you, detective."

We met with my attorney twice before the court date. She went over the details with me, and I wasn't concerned because every detail was etched in my mind. I didn't discuss it with anyone else. I was too embarrassed and felt dirty even thinking about it. No one talked to me about it either. Would I have talked to my dad about it if I had one? What would he have done? It was likely best that I had no dad. I heard the word pedophile mentioned when my mom and aunt were discussing it, but I didn't know exactly what that was. I heard my mom talking about it on the phone to male family members. Snippets of adult conversation that held no meaning for me, but I knew it wasn't good. It was one of the only times I kept quiet and didn't ask my usual barrage of questions.

I did not return to Art School. They offered to let me come for free the next session but my joy and my dreams for that were gone.

The court date arrived and it was a hot humid sticky Jersey day. The slip my grandmother inevitably made me wear, with an undershirt, pants and a blouse, was unbearable. The thin cotton was already sticking to me as we walked in the building. She had put so much starch in it that it was starting to make me itch. My hair, neatly pressed with a hot comb that morning, was already frizzy and escaping the two elastic bands holding the pigtails on either side of my head. The bangs that started out hanging in my eyes were already shrunk with the heat and sweat halfway up my forehead.

When I was called I took a deep breath, and on shaky legs walked to the front of the courtroom.

"Do you swear to tell the whole truth and nothing but the truth, so help you God?"

"I do."

My voice sounded very small and far away to me.

My attorney was talking and I was answering.

"Is that man in the courtroom today?"

"Yes."

"Can you point to him?"

He stared at me with no expression as I pointed to him. My heart was pounding in my ears as I quickly looked away. I thought *he's old. He's older than my mother*. I found that shocking. Why would this old white man try to get me in his car? Did he want to hurt me? Or worse, kill me? Why did he press up against me?

I was talking when the judge in mid-sentence cut me off.

"That is inadmissible," the judge said. "It is not included in your papers to the court."

"But it's true. It happened!!"

I looked at my lawyer. She looked down.

I testified to the truth, the whole truth and nothing but the truth.

The old man with the heinous smile and the eyes of Satan lied.

The verdict was swift. I stood in front of Judge Warlock, my mom on my right and my attorney on the left.

"Little girl, you have a very vivid imagination. You should not make up stories or they will get you in trouble," he said to me.

I was so ashamed, I prayed to God for deliverance. I seriously wanted the floor to give way and swallow me up. My cheeks were on fire, my knees buckled and my mom steadied me. The judge was still talking and leaning towards me but I only heard noise. His finger was wagging and his lips were moving. I was frozen, the only thing moving on me was my eyelashes as I frantically batted back tears. I would not humiliate myself by crying.

To this very day I hate and have a fear of courtrooms. So much so, when I fell like a log over a misplaced cord in the Vegas hotel with the fountains in front, and had to have my disc in my neck replaced, I did not sue them.

"What happened? I asked, "Why did the judge say that to me?"

The detective apologized. My lawyer apologized and looked down. My mom whispered to me as she grabbed my hand.

"Don't you worry honey. You will NEVA see him again."

Her tone sounded very strange. My mother told me the truth that day, I never saw him again.

***

One day, months later, I asked her.

"Do you think he has bothered any other girls since he didn't go to jail, Mommy?"

"Nope. I doubt that."

With her words I was done with the subject and anything that reminded me of it. I locked it in the vault where I put all my unpleasant things.

I tried not to think of his eyes, but it was hard.

It was a bitter and early lesson that truth and justice does not always prevail. That people can get away with lying and labeling me a liar, a pretender, a storyteller.

Dear reader, I know this to be a fact, neither the Dennisses of this world, nor the many people who will in their own brokenness attempt to break and control us, can break you unless you let them.

For me, as long as the sun comes up, and there is music in the world and someone I can help, I'm good.

Judge Warlock, you were so wrong. You humiliated me and violated me for a second time in your courtroom. But you were right as well. I do have a vivid imagination and these days I make a living as a storyteller.

That day was the beginning of my turning Pain into Power.

Still, it was a long time before I could forget his eyes looking at me.

*bitti – Turkish for Finished. Done. Moving on.

PIPPI LONGFELLOW

As I learned from growing up, you don't mess with your grandmother." — Prince William

***

My grandma called anyone who had pets in their house "Nasty and Dirty!" We were not allowed to have pets and we were certainly not allowed to visit anyone who had them. Correction: I had a bird when I was nine. I named her Pippi Longfellow. She was an ordinary blue parakeet, and they are not known for talking, but that did not deter my younger brother. He patiently spent endless hours repeating:

"Hello, hello, hello...hello"

He could not get a single cheep. I, on the other hand, had only to start chit-chatting and she would chatter and chirp away right back at me. Perhaps because I didn't put such intense demands on her. I accepted her limitations and we got along splendidly. Her cage took up most of the corner in my tiny little room, which was little more than a closet. Every morning she would wake me up to the happy sounds of her chirp-chat. To this day, when I hear birds chirping outside my window, I think of Pippi.

It was a Saturday night and we were having family movie night at home complete with popcorn, sarsaparilla soda and my favorite Toll House chocolate chip cookies. I was really excited because the movie was entitled "The Birds" and I was certain to learn something new about Pippi as I was a research fanatic. In fact, my bird was only second to my favorite possession: a set of World Book Encyclopedias. My brother was also interested, thinking he would possibly get tips on how to get the bird to talk. We talked all week about movie night with great anticipation.

Oh, how young and innocent and naive we were. This movie "The Birds" was not at all what we thought and definitely didn't work out the way we planned. Instead, we were spellbound and terrified as the story unfolded. I should have listened to my gut when the music started as I knew it was not for me. I suffered for it, with nightmares all night and sleepwalking.

I woke up the next day to the sound of silence. Opening one eye I called to her.

'Pippi?"

I mimicked her cheeps and chirps.

"Pippi?"

Pippi's cage was empty. I willed myself to calm down and hunted everywhere possible calling her name before logic clicked in place. I froze as it suddenly dawned on me that the door was not open. How could she possibly unlatch the cage and then lock it back again.

"Steven!!! Where is Pippi???? WHERE IS MY BIRD????"

Frantic, I ran from room to room calling out to Pippi. Looking in corners and under beds with a sinking feeling in the pit of my stomach. I raced downstairs to the kitchen, screaming at the top of my lungs:

"PIPPI, PIPPI, PIPPIIIIIIIII!"

"You better stop all that hollerin first thing in the morning!' my grandmother said with a tone that meant you had better put the brakes on and shut the eff up. Although I never heard her curse and with 19 kids she was entitled to cuss.

Lower lip quivering, biting back a flood of emotions, I said miserably:

"I can't find Pippi! I can't find my bird."

"Chile, after that movie last night, I done open up the cage and let his tail fly right out that window."

This was confirmation for me at nine years old what I always suspected that my grandmother was a little bit crazy. But I forgave her because she was born in the 1800s and was old. I also learned the one who has the money and authority has all the power and control.

I started looking for a job the next day to save money so that I too could escape.

My mom offered, but I didn't want another bird.

I woke up the next day in a cold sweat.

THE VAULT OF UNPLEASANT THINGS

I believe it is not an exaggeration to say feet are akin to penises. I'm not referring to the folklore that says the size of a man's hands and feet are an indicator of his penis size.

I can say unequivocally that is simply not true. I know at least two men that have a size 8 shoe with 10 inch penises. I only slept with one of them but I digress.

What I mean is, for me, touching someone's feet requires a level of intimacy that makes me uncomfortable. I have definitely handled more penises than feet. It started in 8th grade when Tom Pence and I played our version of hide and seek: he would hide the lock to my locker down his pants.

In fact, just between us, I'd much rather give a hand job than a foot massage. Well, maybe not to the point of ejaculation, that's by far too much work or is it?

I definitely am not saying I gave Tom Pence a hand job. Besides, a mouth and a grapefruit work infinitely better than a hand. But I impart these random rambling bits of nonsense simply to say we all enjoy different physical attributes. We all have certain preferences, mine happens to be great hands, and feet (if I don't have to touch them).

My friend Allie used to say her husband's feet were so smelly his socks could stand up and run away by themselves when he took them off. He wouldn't have stood a chance with me, that would have been a deal breaker from the get-go. Funny how little things can be deal breakers but red lights flashing and megaphones blaring STOP DO NOT PROCEED can be ignored. As it turned out, she should have run away like those stinky socks. Too bad big hands and smelly feet couldn't tell us something useful like who's a liar and a cheat. We could save ourselves a lot of time and heartache. I do believe; however, penises give us a clue. Now this is just a life lesson according to me, Zelly, I have no scientific data to cite, but a man's penis is a definite clue to his character. All the men who are reading this do not take offense! Allie's husband was outgoing, fun and full of charm because he was a man carrying a big stick. He had one that was too big for his britches, and he wanted to show it off to everyone. My best friend Darlene, on the other hand, had the opposite problem. After years of verbal and physical abuse from her husband she confided in me one day:

"You know, Zelly, I hate to say this, even though I hate him with every breath in my body, but Tom has the tiniest little thing, it's not even the size of my thumb." She lifted up her small hands to demonstrate.

"Whoa!"

I gasped so loud I sucked air down the wrong pipe and went into a wheezing and coughing fit.

"What?????? Say What????? Girl, you have got to be kidding me!"

I guffawed and immediately clapped my hand over my mouth. I stared at her in shock and disbelief, biting back something I'm not sure what. Laughter maybe, but that would be like laughing at someone with some real issues and I'm nothing if not empathetic to the plight of others.

"No, I feel terrible saying it, but I can't stand him! He has made my life and the kids' lives hell.'

"Darlene, it all makes sense to me now! Honey, don't you know a man's self-worth is tied to his penis???"

I don't know if there is research to back me up on that theory, but her husband was a terrible man; very mean, cold and cruel; he was a narcissistic psycho. Was it related to his size? By my logic, neither Mr Big Stuff nor Tom Thumb could have been good mates. One was born to show off and show out, and the other... Well, the less said the better. I like a man with a medium size stick; just enough that he has no messy Napoleonic complex and enough to make you holla nonsensical words when what he's putting down is so damn good. A guy you can laugh with while in awkward crazy positions from the Kama Sutra.

If we haven't met, my name is Zelda and I'm a storyteller. My grandmother used to grumble under her breath and say to no one in particular:

"Zelly, quit telling stories! She ain't nothin but a storyteller!"

To her generation, that was a way of saying you're lying, fibbing or making stuff up. The truth is I have so many stories to tell. So many different loves and lives, and lies as well. Too many experiences to put into one book because you, dear reader, would frankly think like my grandmother – it is all made up.

It was the inspiration of a famous Turkish actor/author, short story writer Engin Akyürek and my husband who, in his infinite wisdom, suggested I write a series of short stories. I have discovered I quite enjoy weaving these little tales that go from the mundane to the miraculous that are my truth and journey. We all sooner or later have to face the truth that what happens to us along the way, the random acts of kindness or love, violence or victimization can foster or shatter our peace. For me, love and peace and a good view outside my office window are what I need most, and I will fight not to be separated from the first two.

I am in my eighth, maybe tenth serious relationship, so I know quite a lot about the subject of loving and being loved. There are so many crazy and exciting levels to loving, don't you think? There's puppy love on one end and unconditional love at the other end, with plenty of subterranean mess, lust and alchemy in between. With each one of those men, I felt certain I had reached the pinnacle, that I had found my Romeo, my Heathcliff – beginning with Dennis. That is why they say Love is Blind and comes equipped with blinders. Each new relationship starts with incredible passion. An all-consuming yearning of such depth, breadth and intensity that I thought, *this is it!*

Wrapped up in a warm exotic cocoon of happy energy I would call my mom and my girlfriends giddy, laughing and dancing with joy!

"I have found the one! He's funny! He's hot! He's kind hearted! He loves kids! He's so sweet! He makes me laugh more than anyone! We can talk for hours! He's this, he's that..."

Fill in the blanks because whatever my heart and soul was craving most at the time, that was what I instinctively drew to me.

This Is. Why. You. Have. To. Be. Intentional. With. Your. Thoughts!

You have to KNOW yourself.

You have to know that the energy you are putting out will attract that very thing to you.

The Baptist preacher performing at my sweet aunt's funeral service in Virginia would twist around, lean sideways and shout out to the congregation when he felt he said something profound:

"AMEN?!!!????"

Each one of these boys-to-men I thought would be the last. You may think I was addicted to falling in love, but truly I wasn't. It wasn't just the promise of my new love adoring me and causing my knees to buckle but also the bond of friendship and camaraderie that enticed me. It wasn't just my elevated heartbeat or the jolts of pleasure in my belly when we were together. It cannot be said that we didn't try hard to make the relationship work, since the shortest was two years and the longest fourteen, but one love story would always end and another begin.

How do we know the truth of love anyway? How do we know the difference between true love, puppy love, summer love, infatuation, love for a reason, a season or a lifetime? Doesn't it all feel the same way initially? How do we know when love is dysfunctional and dangerous? Love stories all have a start in heaven, don't they? Too bad so sad that some end in hell.

Of the seven or so who played such a major role in my life, my first love turned out to be psychotic (you've met Dennis), one was a little bit neurotic, two were liars and cheated, and one had the disease of addiction. Oh, and one was on the down-low and using me as a beard. In other words, he was gay man pretending to be a straight man while having a relationship with a gay man, and trying to convince the world and himself otherwise with a wife. I tend to like my gays straight forward and out of the closet but I ain't mad at him because I was blessed to bypass the toads. These guys were all princes, good men to varying degrees, similar in their compassionate nature and good hearted. I always liked the variety. I knew girls that preferred one type of guy, not me. Three were black, one Hispanic and four were white, but all grew up middle class in different places from different backgrounds, so how did five of them end up in Texas where I live?

Someone once joked that I was the inspiration for the song, *All my exes live in Texas*.

I say *hhmmmph* to that!

***

It was the '70s and I worked for a very prestigious company in Newark, NJ at age twenty-one. I actually loved my work and most of the people I worked with. I took pride in knowing that I was hired as the youngest manager-in-training. My department was responsible for changing the organization from a manual process to a computer process. The analysts created the coding for the program, and my job was to learn the department's existing systems and procedures to help accomplish that. As the assignment was drawing to a close, it occurred to me I could create an additional opportunity for myself that I would enjoy. The higher-ups accepted my proposal, and I created the training manual and conducted the training for the Stocks and Bonds Department of a major company. That company was a vital cornerstone in Newark and was quite progressive for its time. They offered a free hot lunch for all employees and had a workout room, and later on, at my suggestion, even offered women self-defense classes. However, the words *Men* and *Women* were still carved over the massive entrance doors, a reminder of a time in history when the sexes were not allowed to enter together. When I started working, there was still a dress code and women were not allowed to wear pants. Everyone was allowed to indulge their cigarette habit however and curls of smoke were seen wafting in the air from the ashtrays sitting on every desk. Many commented that I just wasted cigarettes, a commentary on the long ash on my burning untouched Newports or Salems. But it was the social thing to do back then.

Who were they to say something anyway, after all, I'd been smoking for nine years and I'd been working making my own money for longer than that, so it was mine to waste. Naturally, I didn't say this out loud as I was trying to heed my grandmother's warning to not let anything that popped into my head fly out of my mouth. Besides, I had a reason for not smoking. No, I wasn't pregnant, that was behind me, and besides, pregnant women smoked and drank back then. It was simply that I was too busy; too focused on trying to get another promotion to smoke.

"Mind your beeswax, Miss Mathilde," I said to one busybody. Back then that was considered a great clapback, the ultimate *put you in your place* comment. Today they just say, "Shut the fuck up bitch" or worse. I'm still not brazen enough to say that to anyone. Besides, no one cursed in my household growing up and good old habits die hard.

That job was very satisfying to me as both a work environment and a social life. I met lots of great friends there. On Fridays we would hang out after work for drinks and lots of belly laughs. There were plenty of great clubs and restaurants in Newark and I spent a total of five years there and built long, varied and meaningful relationships. I even introduced my best friend, Darlene, to her next husband, Dan. He was a great friend of mine and would have me in stitches with his way of laughing with his mouth shaped in an O, like that little emoji.

“Har, har, har. Ahhhh, har, har, har...”

I can still hear the sound of it punctuated by slaps on his thigh. I didn’t date anyone from work myself. I didn’t want the entanglement and potential issues if it didn’t work out and/or interfered with my plans to move up. Besides, I was still scorched from my past intense, all-consuming love affair with Dennis. It was enough that we were all happy, good looking and carefree young people during that time. Our biggest concern was what club we were going to that weekend, and for us girls what to wear. It felt good to just be part of that. Nothing too serious, nothing too deep, that is until I met Jack.

We called him... I don't remember what we called him... lol Jack the Snack or some such nonsense! Only he wasn’t just a snack, he was a full course meal. Several courses, in fact, in a private room with a fabulous wine cellar, in an exclusive mansion catered by a Michelin five-star chef. Yum, that’s how good he looked and, turns out, he was indeed the whole package!

“Zelly, let's go down to DC for the weekend. It’s Howard’s Homecoming and we can visit my cousin Harry over at Georgetown U.”

So, my third cousin from Montclair and her two cousins all tossed our bags in the trunk of my new Mercury Cougar and headed out to take a Girl’s Road Trip from Montclair down to Washington DC. We loved a good campus party, and this weekend was destined to be a good time.

It was an era for great music and time flew past singing our favorite tunes from The Carpenters, Elton John, The Bee Gees, Stevie Wonder, Gloria Gaynor, Eagles, Minnie Riperton, Earth Wind & Fire, Labelle, David Bowie and of course Captain and Tennille. We swung into town confident in our uniform of tight jeans, platforms and skimpy halter tops. I had on my favorite 6" pink patent leather platform shoes with white polka dots, bell bottoms slung low on my hips and a pale pink gauzy halter that showed off my belly button. I had not worn a bra in years, but I passed the pencil test.

When Harry walked out with his roommate Jack, our chatter came to a screeching halt just like in a romcom. The four of us girls looked at one another and looked back at him. He was mesmerizing! *Babeee,* his walk – no, make that his stride – had all eyes like laser beams on him. Tight jeans over lean powerful muscular thighs and calves. Long, lean torso, and nice pecs in a tight tee. Just the way I like it. I didn't care for bulky weightlifter types. I liked my men lean, long and hard. As he got closer, I noted he had long lashes, but they were curly as if he used a lash curler. Hazel eyes. Short curly 'fro. Whew! He was a fine, fine specimen of a man. Damn he was hot!

Jack and I locked eyes and I just stared, and he stared back. I think I said *Hi* to Harry and hugged him. Maybe, maybe not. We went through introductions, and we babbled something about meeting up after we checked into our hotel.

I listened to my cousin and her cousins gush on and on about him all the way back to the hotel, while I thought about him.

By the time we arrived in the room my mind was made up and I blurted out.

"Honeeeee, you girls can talk about Jack all you want, but I'm going after him. In fact, I'm going to make him mine. Everyone okay with that?"

"What!?"

"What about Harry??? Isn't that going to feel weird, going out with his best friend?"

"Why??? Harry was... well, Harry was childhood puppy love," I said with a big Cheshire Cat grin.

"Childhood?? Zelly, you were just dating Harry in high school!"

"Okay, but we went on our first date at twelve! We were kids! Actually, it did start as kids! We were bride and groom in a Tom Thumb wedding at nine and had our first kiss. Haaaa! I told you we were kids!"

"I thought you were thinking about trying to see if there was still something between you two?"

"Hhhmmmm, let me check..." Tapping my temple and tilting my head to one side. "Aahhhhh, nope! I'm not thinking that. Besides we broke up because he cheated on me with my sorry, sly, sneaky excuse for a cousin!" Today you know she would be known as a THOT (that ho over there).

"You of all people, Ginger, know exactly what happened."

And that, dear reader, is how the story of Jack and Zelda began, but I'm getting ahead of myself.

I turned down scholarships and acceptance to Ivy League schools in favor of working and attending school in the evenings. I know, I know, you'll understand why later AND I do not recommend that route. At any rate, it was a relatively short walk from my employment to the college campus. On the days I had class I'd commute to work via bus and train, rather than drive since parking was both an inconvenience and a nightmare. The bus took me 80% of the way there before I'd transfer to the "train". It was little more than a version of a trolley with one giant side door that slid open for passengers to enter or exit before clackety-clacking rocking from side-to-side down the old tracks. I was anal, and conscious of measuring and minimizing motion for maximum outcomes, always choosing to sit if possible right across from the opening door. I could be the first to dash out and speed away unhindered. More importantly, I could avoid the occasional contact with someone as they would brush by. After Dennis, I hated even the unintentional unavoidable contact of anyone. I would jump out of my skin if someone approached me suddenly or touched me, especially from behind. So, I would sit motionless in my own little safe spot and watch others or read or simply think.

There were mostly white middle-aged businessmen in suits with briefcases, and a mix of white secretaries. I only realize that now looking back at it. My family was a rainbow of Italian, Scandinavian, French, and African, I really didn't talk or think in terms of color. I thought about how I didn't understand the conversations I had with one of my bosses. Iris was a tall, good-looking, blonde, first-generation German woman with a quirky husband who liked to vacuum the hallway outside their apartment naked. Surely it was enough that he would be out there vacuuming but nekkid??? I rolled my eyes when she told me and asked her what if the neighbors caught him.

She shrugged and said, "That's his problem! He's such a kook."

I wondered about a woman who would marry a kook and then tell all his secrets. But what really annoyed me was she was always saying things like:

"You can tell she's Jewish!"

"You always know when they're Polish"

"You know that one is...."

She eventually pursued a friendship with me and my husband, and we'd have couples' nights. When I felt comfortable enough, I finally got up the nerve to come right out and ask her:

"Iris, how do you know they're Polish or Jewish, they just look white to me?"

She looked at me with a puzzled look on her face that I couldn't decipher. Did she think I was ignorant or unsophisticated? She went on carefully describing levels of intelligence, nose shapes and sizes of ethnic groups. Her sentences were filled with stereotypes, at best, and plenty of racial slurs. As I listened intently, she warmed up even more, mistaking my interest for consent. I wondered what she thought about me, but I kept mum. I didn't trust her to be that good of a friend not to try and penalize me at work if I criticized her or said what I felt.

I thought about Iris and others at work on the train ride. Sometimes I would sit and watch the people getting on and off. I could see pain and worry etched in the faces of some, and others wore a mask plastered in place to hide their true feelings. In my head I would write the stories of their lives. I thought the woman with her bangs cut too short was suffering from anxiety and depression. The woman in the shapeless nondescript clothing, and the sad yellowing gray strands escaping from her hat, had gone through recent trauma. I could feel the heaviness of their spirits. It was a relatively quiet ride without the usual banter and noises that were on the bus, even if it was only the bus driver greeting everyone good morning. It was fourteen minutes of peace before the start of my busy day.

This day started out no different from any other. I got off the bus and sprinted down the stone steps to the old train. There was one already there with people piling in and I decided to wait five minutes for the next one. As I entered, I saw a man was sitting in the window next to the seat I wanted across from the door. I noted he was middle-aged, harmless looking, a brown leather briefcase in his lap, he glanced up at me and smiled as I sat down.

As usual, I was deep in thought and musings. As the train pulled into the next stop, the man suddenly jumped up with his briefcase in his left hand and shoved the right hand up my skirt and grabbed me by the________.

Shocked, she jerked towards the door just in time to see the bottom of a dirty worn shoe, the back of a dark blue suit and straight blonde hair leaping out the door. The doors slid shut, leaving just the sound of clackety-clack as the train wobbled in innocence down the tracks.

She felt her stomach lurch and felt sick. She could hear her heart pounding as blood roared through her ears. She sat still as a corpse, hoping to disappear. Her eyes darted around at other passengers, certain that someone else had witnessed it and would be staring at her.

Why? she asked.

How could someone do this to another person? For what reason? To humiliate? To get his rocks off? Was he a pervert? Had he done it before? Why target her? Did he know he was going to do it when he looked at her? Did he decide before then?

Had he seen her before? Did he have a wife? Daughter? Sister?

Was there something she did? Was it her scent? Why would a total stranger grab her in such a disgusting manner? Why did she attract this to herself?

Why did older boys shove their hands up her skirt when she was six?

She thought back to when she skipped first grade at Rand School and found herself in second grade with three boys who stayed back twice. She was small for six years old and, at eight and nine, they towered over her. She was terrified of them, especially nine-year-old Timmy, who always walked up behind her desk and made disgusting sucking noises in her ear while whispering:

"I'm going to get you."

She dreaded the end of the day when they had to get their coats from the cloakroom. A dark, narrow space with hooks on the wall where bad boys did bad things to you. She thought it was the price of being popular, because on Valentine's Day she got more cards on her desk than anyone else. And so she kept quiet and told no one. She suffered in her own silence.

Besides, on the bright side she would rather be noticed for being pretty and popular rather than smart and a tattletale. She hated when kids called her "Brainiac". What does it matter if you're reading at a high school level to a six-year-old? You just want to be liked and accepted, and not mocked. She learned to hide her brains as best she could behind a silly bubbly personality, only taking them out when she really needed them around adults. She quickly learned no one likes a know-it-all child and, later on an adult, who is always right.

Even teachers scolded her saying:

"Zelda! Give someone else a chance to answer a question."

At six she started having nightmares. She was terrified of the dark, shadowy figures, small spaces and certain sounds, like the themes from The Twilight Zone and Outer Limits. She dreamt people were sitting on her, suffocating her. Her arms would get stuck behind her back and the pain was excruciating. She thought about what her grandmother said about the dead trying to communicate with her and she was afraid to fall asleep. She would read all night under the covers with a flashlight.

The sun comes up and we think we are fine. We struggle to adapt and survive, doing our best to get by day-to-day. Do we accomplish what we think we are accomplishing? Although I tried, my mouth still betrayed me and I said anything that popped in my head, and both my mom and grandmother didn't hesitate to remind me. Once at dinner I said something that caused my grandmother to hurl the large serving spoon, she was about to dig into the mashed potatoes, straight at me.

"You too fresh!"

Like an expert knife thrower, and living up to her nickname, Annie Oakley, she nailed her target. Shocked, I was surprised to taste blood and feel what was a piece of chipped tooth on my tongue. Jumping up from the table both stunned and hurt, I ran upstairs to my room thinking *dark thoughts*. I had never been hit before. My mother did not believe in spanking her children. She would never allow anyone to touch us. On the other hand, I don't remember getting hugs either growing up.

So, when this degenerate stranger violated me in that way, when he invaded my private space and place in such a disgusting way, I didn't tell anyone. I was too embarrassed and ashamed. Besides, what was the point? What could anyone do or say that would make a difference?

I went to the library and checked out eight books. Books were unconditional love. They weren't puppy love, or summer love or seasonal love; they lasted a lifetime. Reading, I could experience someone else's emotions when mine were too exhausting to handle. Besides, no one died, and it would take far more to kill my spirit. That belonged to me alone, and I alone had control. If I controlled my thoughts, I controlled my feelings. So, I put the thought of that stranger on the train where I put all the other painful thoughts, in the *Vault of Unpleasant Things* and locked it shut. By the way I hate trump for saying ..grab her by the "p___y".

The next week I met Jack.

I'm smiling just thinking about it.

***

JACK AND ZELLY

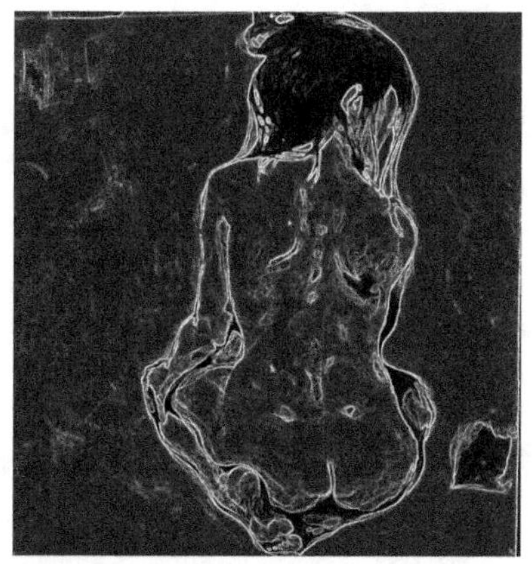

"At night, I open the window and ask the moon to come and press its face against mine. Breathe into me. Close the language-door and open the love-window. The moon won't use the door, only the window." – Rumi

***

Jack's family was well known in the political scene in DC, and I adored his dad who was by far the best politician I've ever met.

Jack and I met on a weekend Girls' Trip to DC and it was love at first sight. Lord, I just wanted to breathe the same air that man was breathing. Inhale the scent of his cologne and watch the same sky that his brown eyes gazed upon. Every time I see Michael Ealy in the Beyonce *Halo* video I am reminded of Jack.

It was so hard being separated by a three-hour car drive. So, after nine months we did the only logical illogical thing we could do and jumped the broom. Well, not literally, we didn't know anything about that particular tradition.

Our wedding was magnificent. Spectacular, in fact. We had regional celebs and politicians, and it was the wedding of the year, covered by the local society columns and *Jet* magazine. People talked about it for years. We were the hot, new, power couple in the making.

When Jack moved in, I counted thirty-two designer sweaters on hangers with Chinese Laundry tags on them. There were too many expensive starched shirts to count, along with suits, slacks, jackets, shoes and ties. My mouth dropped. He was a college senior at the time. During a time when I was spending $30 on a top, he was spending that on one tie. Wow just wow.

We did our share of steaming up the windows of his sexy red sports car when I visited, but we both decided to wait until marriage for actual intercourse. Jack and I were so head over heels back then, smiling into each other's eyes was our favorite pastime. Holding hands, arms around one another, we walked at the same pace. He was a super-hot guy with a really sweet, crooked smile and hazel eyes that twinkled when he was happy. He was also very arrogant and walked with the confidence of a man who knows he is from a prominent family. In another time and place he would have been called an *uppity negro* or its derogatory moniker *uppity nigger*. All of my girlfriends were a little in awe of him and intimidated by him. Yes, he was arrogant, but I was so in love with him that his arrogance did not matter to me – besides, it was not directed at me. I decided it was his armor, like one of his many designer suits he put on to go out in the world and try to slay dragons. What I loved most of all was his intellect, and the fact that we looked so exceptionally good together. But I sigh as I say that, since all was not as great as it looked from the outside, or the inside for that matter. You see, we were missing a key ingredient in this love goulash, the meat! Neither one of us were that crazy about love making. Frankly, I never even had an orgasm and I started to think I was that dreaded word back then, *frigid*. I did however crave affection from him more so than I ever had with anyone else. Sadly, the more I wanted it the more he pulled away, but on the other hand we could talk for hours. Sometimes when we came home, we could sit in the car for over an hour just chatting away before one of us would *say, Guess we should continue this inside*, and laugh.

***

“Stop it! Zelly, why are you hanging onto my neck?”

I heard that a zillion times. I tried to snuggle at night, and he'd push me away. I spent most nights with silent tears rolling down my crumpled face. I told no one. How could I? Outwardly, things looked hunky dory. Lol, I cannot hear that phrase anymore without hearing the delightful and fabulous Kathy Hilton of the *Beverly Hills Housewives* show saying "Who is hunky dory???" with that incredibly funny puzzled look on her face. She was responding to someone declaring everything was "hunky dory".

Who indeed is hunky dory? lol

We both worked, and on the weekends got together with other couples from my job, including my boss Iris and her husband, to hang out and play cards. We both loved music and when I could drag him out on the dance floor I would, and we would get caught up in the gyrations of our bodies to the beat; all the while smiling at one another and laughing. I was partially laughing because I thought he looked like he was performing a rain dance, but you have to keep some things to yourself. I was learning my mom and grandma were right, everything that pops into your head shouldn't fly out of your mouth.

We laughed a lot. We cracked ourselves up laughing at each other's conversation. But cracks started to appear in the foundations. We were not making enough money to satisfy his needs, his standard of living and, because he dropped out in his senior year, he couldn't get the job he wanted. He had no place to wear all those designer suits and after two years of marriage his parents made an offer he couldn't refuse.

"Why don't you and Zelda come back to DC live with us and we will pay for you both to finish school."

Uhhhh, no ma'am!

But I didn't decline right away. I honestly thought long and hard about it, and we both spent hours discussing the pros and cons. After all, we were still in love.

***

When I first laid eyes on my mother-in-law I thought, *wow, what a truly lovely, graceful woman smiling at me*. I secretly wished she was my mom.

"Hello Zelda! Aren't you a pretty little thang."

She drawled in that sugary soft voice while looking me up and down and turning me as if we were about to play a game of *Pin the Tail on the Donkey*.

"Ma hairdresser could do wonders with yo hair."

She used two syllables for the word hair. *Hay-ya*.

I thought. People raved about my *hay-ya* all the time! I was in magazines for my *hay-ya*. I had that chemically straightened bouncin' and behavin' Prell girl *hay-ya*.

No, I would not, could not move in with them. I wouldn't look good in the coiffed *hay-ya* of a Washington socialite. I had seen *The Stepford Wives* and I had zero interest in starring in a version called *The High Society Housewives from the Potomac*. (note I wrote this before the popular Bravo show)

So, Jack packed up his neatly hangered thirty-two sweaters, and freshly Chinese laundered shirts, and moved back to DC.

Without me.

That final day we looked into each other's tear-filled eyes, and I noticed again, as if for the first time, how long and curly his lashes were. He was looking at me with such love I was regretting and rethinking my decision.

In the end we parted with the reassurance that we'd talk daily and write letters, and weekend visits were planned until we were back together when he graduated. Afterall, it was less than a year.

Did we have farewell sex before he left?

I think we did.

***

1300 Dates

"I'm just a soul whose intentions are good,

Oh Lord please don't let me be misunderstood" –song by The Animals

***

Someone tell me exactly why big, huge butts that are disproportionate to the body are the new beauty status? Please write in and tell me who started this shit. You can send it to my Dear Zelly page. Why the need to have surgery and/or makeup to resemble a plastic doll with a shaved nose, big eyes, and permanently pursed bee stung lips? Of course, my mom felt that way about afros and miniskirts and platform shoes so I guess I would have to be young and hip to know the answer to that. I am hip but older. Is the reason women take pictures in bathroom mirrors of their boobs and booties and abs sucked in, is because they now fully understand that this body has an expiration date? We have had many trends throughout the years that caused me to look at my photos and say:

What the hell was I thinking??!

But I was never that sexually free in my past to flaunt my butt in a sexy pose. I come from a demurer generation where those in the know posed with toes pointed at ten and two. Besides, at 34-24-35 I didn't have much to show off. These hips came much later in life, and I am always surprised to see them along with the weight of these twin peaks. The perky breasts that used to point north, now they point southeast and southwest. Interesting how fat distribution is different as you age. You will learn this.

Does the music inspire the style and define beauty, or vice versa? The glorification of body parts has always found its way into culture through music, but I miss the double entendre and sexual innuendos of songs of bygone era like *My Big 10" Inch,* written by Fred Weismantel and recorded by Bull Moose Jackson. Then rerecorded by Aerosmith.

There were always sexy songs like *Sexual Healing,* and *I found my thrill on Blueberry Hill,*

Then there were the popular goofy songs like:

The Name Game... Zelly Zelly bo belly banana fana fo Felly fee fie mo Melly...

Yakety Yak (don't talk back) and *That Charlie Brown he's a clown.*

In the 2000's we have WAP WAP WAP and BOP BOP BOP. If you don't know the acronyms, Google them.

I miss fun songs. But I still dance and twerk to Cardi B and DaBaby! Regardless and in spite of the explicit lyrics!

***

I was in the elevator going up to the fourteenth floor to see my uncle Clyde who I just adored. I heaved a sigh of relief because nobody was in with me when just before the doors shut a tall man stepped in with a small black bag. I instantly recognized it as being a camera bag.

"You should be a model"

Momentarily distracted from my battle with claustrophobia, I paused for a moment thinking, what does he want from me?

"I do model" followed by "I'm not interested."

"Interested in what?" he laughed.

I strode off the elevator at floor 14, tossed my hair and turning left said over my shoulder

"Bye"

Somehow, I found myself with that photographer, in the penthouse of the Clinton Towers, listening to songs I did not like, shooting photos for submission to Penthouse magazine.

But enough of my musings about music, I am just feeling nostalgic because my husband Jack and I loved those old songs, but there was no more Jack and me. Jack, who I had fallen for at first sight, had fallen right off my bed and my radar.

***

Jack saw her before she saw him. His breath caught in his Adam's apple just for half a second when her eyes met his. She was beautiful. The thought flashed in his head: *my mom would approve of her*. She had hair like his mom's, and his mom's coloring and chiseled features. As he strode towards her, he had to remind himself not to be nervous. When he was nervous, he stuttered. He spent so many years overcoming that stigma. Not many people knew that about him, not even his best friend, Harry.

He met Harry at University as a roommate, and they bonded. Zelda was Harry's first girlfriend when they were twelve but their history went back to childhood when Harry's dad was having an affair with Zelda's mother. Harry had described Zelda to him, but she was an angel in person and he could not stop gazing intently in her warm brown eyes. He was drowning in her eyes. Did he shake her hand when greeting her? Did he stutter?

The four girls – or was it three? – were walking away from them when she turned and looked over her shoulder at him and smiled. A smile that promised it was going to be an interesting night. Maybe this was the one.

It lasted two years.

***

After Jack, I was emotionally lazy and spiritually spent. I was confused. I was definitely not interested in falling in love again. A few months later I dated thirteen different guys in one month. It was a fun and exhilarating but challenging at the same time. Like a statistician I had to keep a journal of what I said to whom. I also kept a list of what I did with whom.

Just for the fun of it I vetted every one of them and not even for potential boyfriend material. As Cyndi said, "Girls just wanna have fun!" and I was competing with myself to have the most fun ever.

Just for the hell of it, I judged them. I judged on background, intellect, style, personality, politics, status, affability, spirituality, sexuality, sensuality and whether they had a charitable nature and a vision for the future. Oh, and the one I had sex with I rated him on whether I had an orgasm or whether I had to fake it. I wrote it down in journal. I believed in journaling way back then. Later on, I had the grace to be embarrassed when DT found my journal.

Antoine was funny, outgoing and co-anchor for a local TV station. We went out several times and we almost reached couple status, but he was not kind to others. He was not an unkind man. I even brought him home and we slept in the same bed. I was bothered by his lack of compassion and empathy.

I went to the ballet to see *Swan Lake* at Lincoln Center with Vincent, who was a sweet, sweet guy who worked for Prudential in a different department, on a different floor but he just didn't ring my bell. It was a great date and when we left the performance, I was craving something very specific, a dirty martini up, a medium New York strip steak and pomme frites (French for shoestring fries), a spinach salad (with mushrooms, boiled egg, and warm bacon salad dressing), and a chocolate mousse. And wouldn't you know, right across the street from Lincoln Center was a restaurant that had all of that! He was the first guy I met who loved the ballet and the opera. He asked me to go to Pagliacci, but I said no. I did not want him falling in love with me when I knew nothing further could happen.

Big T was a radio DJ in NYC who I met at a party in Manhattan. He invited me to go see the Pointer Sisters show at Radio City and come to their after party at The Waldorf Astoria. I definitely went out with him as they were my favorite girl group of the moment. I laughed and chatted with June and Anita – much to my delight and had a wonderful magical time. We never had a second date either. No chemistry, he was like going out with a friend, no not a friend, an acquaintance.

Ralph took me to see the movie *Apocalypse Now* and I fell asleep ten minutes in. Afterwards we went out to eat at the famous Tavern on the Green and I only picked at my food. He's the one I slept with for a dumb reason, I felt bad wasting his money.

I recall being voted Queen of Flirts in HS and most likely to give blue balls.

I was unintentionally living up to that perception again.

***

Monet not Manet

Always iron your clothes and have clean underwear on. In case you have an accident and have to go to the hospital.

– Grandma Jackson 1894-1994

***

My hubby said to me this morning in that deadpan reserved way of his:

"Sweetie, you have the Simone Biles of vaginas."

I laughed my tush off! I laughed so long and hard I was doubled over, causing him to blush and say:

"Zelly, you crazy."

Over 500 people signed my yearbook and nearly every single one of them mentioned the word *crazy*. Even one of my favorite teachers wrote, "Zelda your spirit will forever roam the halls, driving your teachers into a state of mania".

What the eff? I thought I was the best-behaved student ever. I went to a private school that you had to test into. I skipped a grade. I was raised to be polite and well mannered. I was never sent to detention nor got expelled nor into any trouble. I must have been a nice person.

When I was fifteen my friend Holly's parents invited me to join them at a dinner party at Yogi Berra's house. To this day my favorite chicken recipe is the one I got from Mrs. Berra. Would they have invited me if I was crazy? So why did my teacher say that? It just goes to show your perception of yourself and how others perceive you is not always the same.

That, dear reader, is what sometimes gets us on the wrong side of trouble. Perception versus reality. That is also a reason to be very aware of yourself and the message you are unintentionally sending others. It can set you up for success or something less.

***

I had been flying to St Thomas in the Virgin Islands since I was sixteen. The first time I flew alone and met up with my uncle and his friends during the April Carnival. After that I went to Carnival every year, sometimes going with my mom or my girlfriend, Stacy. My uncle's friend, Gary, worked for Mr Baldwin, a very powerful and wealthy man. I often stayed at one of his homes since Gary was a caretaker of one of his estates. It was such a magical beautiful place on the tippy-top of a hill with a 360-degree breathtaking view. The villa was surrounded by lush tropical foliage and statues imported from Italy. One guesthouse flanked the pool and the stone steps leading up to the main house. In the guest house I stayed at, the bedroom, living room, dining area and library were built around the pool. In the library, over the fireplace hung a five-million-dollar painting by my favorite artist – Monet. In the quiet of the night under the huge expanse of twinkling stars I would marvel at the lights that shown on the Italian statues as I glided past. It was a divine setting like in the movies. I breathed deeply my lungs filling with the spectacular beautiful hibiscuses and fragrant flowers that I didn't know their names. I floated past the green foliage and statuesque palms. It was just incredible, and my island boyfriend and I would pretend it was our own little slice of heaven in faraway Italy.

Oh my god, those were some good times.

I would meet the owner, Mr. B, on several occasions over the next ten years, but I was shocked when I actually received a letter from him that year.

***

1982

My dear Zelda,

I have enjoyed my encounters with you over the years. I find you both a smart and delightful young woman. I need people like yourself working in my jewelry store and so I would like to offer you a position in sales.

I hope this correspondence finds you and your family in great health.

Sincerely

Mr. Baldwin

***

Dear Mr. Baldwin,

I am so flattered that you would think so highly of me but I am not a salesperson. I hate selling anything. In fact as a Girl Scout I didn't even want to sell cookies, and everyone wants girl scout cookies. I found it too embarrassing to ask. so I will have to politely refuse your kind offer.

I look forward to seeing you on my next trip.

Yours truly

Zelda Taliaferro

***

Dear Zelda,

I hope my letter finds you in good health. To your last correspondence I say Nonsense as I am a great judge of character, and you are a natural salesman. People will buy because you have looks, class and a great personality. I'm offering the job as well as car and lodging at one of my properties for free.

Sincerely

Mr. B

***

Dear Mr. B

I love St Thomas and therefore I am willing to give it a try since you believe in me. However, in order to come I would need a plane ticket and $1000. to purchase clothing and finalize some things here.

Yours truly,

Zelda

***

Dear Zelda,

Enclosed please find a check for $1000 and a first-class ticket. I look forward to seeing you.

Sincerely

Mr. B

***

I hugged my mom, my brother, and Stacy tight at the airport as they saw me off. *Don't cry for me Argentina*, I sang while walking away, blowing kisses and waving to them. They stood in a little huddle together that caused a lump in my throat, and so I turned and hurried away with tears streaming. But I was also excited. I couldn't wait to get there. I didn't look back.

I was leaving my boyfriend, Gene, back home. Gene was a slightly neurotic sweet who wouldn't hurt a fly kind of guy. He was a taxi driver by night and a struggling actor by day. I didn't mind and fully supported his dream, but it was time for me to move on because the relationship was exhausting. So, when I said goodbye to our little studio in the Chelsea section of Manhattan, it was bittersweet.

My island boyfriend couldn't wait for me to arrive either. We had been seeing one another for the past three years when I would visit the island or when he would come to visit his family in Connecticut. In between, we wrote letters to one another all the time and an occasional phone call. A call could easily cost $50, making it unaffordable for us. He lived in St Thomas but traveled on ships to foreign places that I would dream about going to visit with him.

I was to stay in one of the hotels Mr. B owned that was temporarily closed while undergoing renovation. My island guy asked me to stay with him, but he had three male roommates and, after my past experience with Dennis and his roommates, I declined. Not that he was anything like Dennis; in fact, they were totally different – starting with the obvious. Dennis was 6' 7", black and obsessed with nothing except sports and me. Sting was 5' 7", wavy blonde hair, with smiling green eyes and was a ship mechanic who raced motorcycles. He was a carefree spirit like me with varied interests. That was our connection. This could possibly move our *Summer Island Love Story* into something more serious, more permanent.

There is nothing like leaving behind the gray skies and bare trees of Newark and arriving on an island. I had to change planes in Puerto Rico which I always disliked. We disembarked outside and walked down a narrow passageway. I felt the cold cement of the building on the left on my bare arm as I leaned away from the outstretched arms of men behind the fence on the right. It was filled with men who seemed fresh out of the bowels of prison hell. They were reaching out, making creepy kissy sounds and lewdly whistling, and calling out to come to them in Spanish. I didn't speak the language, but I knew what "Ahhhh, que linda" meant and the rest sounded very obscene.

***

I arrived in St Thomas on a blissful sunshiny day and took a cab to the hotel. Since the grounds were closed there was only me and a security guard at the reception desk. I was on the first floor in the room immediately behind the reception desk and office. It was just a room and a balcony; nothing spectacular but nice, and the hotel was right on the beach on a secluded nook of the island. There was just the hotel and several cottages that were also being renovated. I had a fifteen-minute drive into town and work, so I was ecstatic and happy that Mr. B had given me my own car as well.

I spent my first few days jumping on the back of Sting's motorcycle, my arms wrapped tight around his waist as we raced up and down the sun filled green hills of the island, on our way to some lazy fun in the sun. During the nights, my legs were wrapped tight around his waist and filled with the most amazing love making ever. He was very, very well endowed and we made love for hours. He made me forget all about the insane misadventure that started my arrival there.

I made great money and had zero bills! Mr. B was right. I was a salesperson – I started at a tiny little counter in the back of the store where the cheap items that didn't sell were placed. After three weeks Mr. B called me to his office.

"What are you doing, angel?? he asked in amazement. The counter you are at was doing an average of $300 a week and you are averaging $4000 a week. We are promoting you."

I have never been happier, I felt so carefree I can't explain the blissful state I was in. I as a wordsmith cannot find the words to adequately describe what I was feeling. I was delirious. My days were filled with so much fun. I hardly felt like I was working, and the nights were a blur of parties and hot sex.

One night, after a night of way too many drinks, Sting dropped me off in my hotel room. The guard was sleeping so we tiptoed past him, and I kissed Sting at the door saying,

“Do you mind, baby? I am exhausted and besides we both have to work in a few hours?”

The instant my head hit the pillow I passed out on top of the covers in a haze of rum punches and exhaustion.

She awakened to that sick, scary sensation you get in the pit of your stomach. She opened her eyes to see a man stealthily crawling at the foot of the bed towards her. His eyes locked on hers, making her shriek with terror. Over and over and over and over. She was hysterical choking on her own saliva and snot as she stared into his not soon forgotten yellow eyes.

The guard later told the police that I let out so many blood-curdling screams that he did not come to my aid because he thought I was being murdered. Listening to him, I just buried my face in Sting’s chest and collapsed in his arms.

That is how I came to stay with island boyfriend Sting until the hotel was completed and safe to move back there. We had the time of our lives and even made plans for when we were bored of being there or ready to move on. We would travel to South America. We would ride his motorcycle on the open roads, and I would take photos and write stories and submit them to *Life* magazine and *National Geographic*. Next, we would go to Barcelona since he could easily find work on boats off the coast.

***

Mr. B had a global Rolodex of famous and wealthy friends, and lucky for me he asked me to escort him to all kinds of social events. I got to select whatever jewelry I wanted to wear when I accompanied him, and so I would adorn myself in half a million dollars' worth of diamonds. Sting's roommate, Freddie, was a cop and once they were on security duty at a hotel where me and Mr. B attended a fancy event.

"Damn!"

He looked at me with sparkling eyes, or was it the reflection of the diamonds?

"We three could escape off the island and sell and live off those diamonds!" Freddie joked.

The three of us got along great, and had settled into a routine, when one day we had a guest. Evelyn Champagne King arrived. She was just coming off tour and knew Freddie and staying for a while on St Thomas. She and I grew up on the East Coast, so we had that in common. Her presence was a huge deal on that little island, and when we walked into the nightclubs the DJ would instantly play her songs.

Eventually Evelyn left, the hotel renovations were completed, and I moved back to the hotel. No particular reason. I still adored Sting and we saw each other daily; that is until the night when I went to the club solo and met DT.

Ahhh, DT

My pelvic bones slammed into his with such force they melded rather than broke. His teeth hit mine and I tasted just the tiniest bit of blood.

***

The Story of DT

"This is a wonderful day. I've never seen this one before."

– Maya Angelou

***

My pelvic bones slammed into his with such force they melded rather than broke. His teeth hit mine and I tasted just the tiniest bit of blood. His lips and his mouth were sucking the very air out of me. I relaxed into him, actually I melted into him and our bones became one. Our skin, where connected, was on fire.

As you know I moved to the St Thomas, Virgin Islands with a job offer that included a free apartment and free car. At 28 I was truly living my best life, surrounded by nature's finest beauty, and I had never been so carefree. My apartment was on the beach and every day I awoke to white sands, blue, blue water and sky, and every day I gratefully stepped outside, stretched out my arms, threw my head back and let the sun kiss my skin.

Today was different. It was the day after the night I met DT.

At first sight DT took my breath away. My boyfriend, Sting, was doing security work with his friend, Freddie, a cop with the police department, so I went to the dance club alone.

I met DT. But I said that.

I noticed him as soon as I walked in the club – at the bar surrounded by women. I headed straight to the dance floor and, with eyes closed, started getting into the groove of the music.

"Boy meets girl and love, love is on its way..." sung by Haircut 100

“Can I have this dance, Zelda?”

Startled, my eyes shot open to stare into his. He was so polite. His eyes were green and sparkling. I felt a jolt of pleasure. His eyes were so seductive.

“How do you know my name?”

It flashed through my mind what an old-fashioned thing for him to say. This was the 1980's not the 1890's

That was the beginning of the story of Zelda and DT.

***

But Zelly, you are not ready to share their story just yet. Wait a little while.

***

SWEET SIXTEEN

***

Zelly raced up the driveway and flung open her mom's back door. The words *I'm home* had barely left her lips when she came to a halt. Her arms froze in mid air, her sandals as if crazy glued to the floor, she stood immobile. More shock and surprise, if that was possible, showed in her voice.

"What are you doing *here*!!!???"

...she asked incredulously of the nineteen-year-old guy sitting in her mom's kitchen.

His big, chocolate eyes stared at her as if she was water in a desert, he replied without hesitation.

"I came to collect what belongs to me."

She was struck at how an accent that was music to her ears on the Virgin Islands seemed odd and out of place in her mom's New Jersey kitchen. He said those EXACT words and all these years later she recalled them exactly how they were said.

There are milestones that change the course of our lives forever and this day might've been the actual start of my adult life. In fact, it may just be the biggest game changer of all the many crazy, wackadoodle and exciting adventures life had in store for me.

Taking a few shallow breaths, I stepped back until I was out the back door and glanced at – or perhaps just smelled – the rain still glistening on the grass.

***

It was the first day of Spring Break and I was beyond excited to be flying for the first time. Chattering nonstop on the thirty-minute ride to the Newark Airport, I was pumped up on pure adrenaline when we pulled up to Terminal C. Jumping out the car, I told my mom and hugged my brother goodbye, and walked inside. A blast of cold air greeted me. My toe, then heel hit the floor like a model on a Paris runway. I strode through Newark Airport fresh out the beauty parlor – hair swinging. I mimicked the walk I saw of the Pan Am stewardesses. My nearly leather no-name shoulder bag, filled with emergency coins for a phone booth when I arrived, reassuringly bumped against my hip. I carried a small suitcase in my right hand, my mom's light blue overnight Samsonite. So I walked, eyes darting scanning for signs, all the while pretending I was a seasoned traveler not a skinny sixteen-year-old.

I probably should have let my mom and little brother walk me to the gate and wait with me, but I was afraid of teary goodbyes. You'd think I'd be used to goodbyes from my trips to the farm every summer, but something about people waving and looking at me always choked me up.

I found my way to the gate just in time to board. I located my seat as requested in the smoking section, which was a precious few rows in the rear of the plane. I'd snuck three cigarettes out of my grandmother's pack of Salems in her top drawer, hidden between tiny floral printed underpants. Sitting down I thought better of lighting up; knowing they'd likely be stale as she rarely smoked and I'd get nauseous. I was comforted just knowing they were there in my bag, wrapped in a small piece of tin foil, just in case. My eyes confirmed the whereabouts of the closest bathroom. I leaned forward to check the pocket of the seat in front of me, satisfied the dark blue paper bag was just where my uncle Mitch said it would be. My mind wandered in a million directions and random thoughts drifted like the smoke swirling above me. I sat breathing normally and gazing since I was little with my usual intensity at the people around me.

I was extremely excited about this trip, which thankfully overrode my fear of heights at that moment, although my empty stomach did betray me and the dark blue bag came in handy shortly after takeoff. The last plane I flew in was at the Palisades Park boardwalk – a purple miniature that flew out at right angles from a huge pole. That didn't go well; as I recalled closing my eyes. When I saw the top of a building an overwhelming irrational fear and feeling of powerlessness seized my belly, causing me to throw up and pass out at the same time. Not one to give up, I was talked into a Ferris wheel ride which resulted in borrowing a friend's sweater to hide the wet spot on my pants afterwards. Oh well, so I had to cross amusement park rides off my list of things I was capable of, although I disliked admitting it. But I always came home with a prize because I was great at games! I always had a good eye and a steady hand, and my favorite was shooting the steady stream of water through the hole to move your horse along in the horse track game.

I turned my thoughts to my trip and what awaited me. I was only mildly concerned that I only had $20 folded up neatly and secure in the pocket of my tight hip-hugging jeans. I became conscious of the – about a quarter inch of fat bubbling over my jeans. I sighed, feeling uncomfortable and wishing this size 6 wasn't so dang tight. I pondered why I couldn't seem to get rid of that annoying quarter inch but felt much luckier than my friend, Terry. She had to lie flat on the bed, as a result of her obsession with candy and cake, to wiggle and grunt her way into zipping up her size 8. I wondered how Lorie could stand the extra 6 inches that spilled over her size 12 jeans, leaving a healthy pocket of fat below her belt as well. I never thought of her as being fat or overweight, I simply didn't understand why she didn't buy the right size. It just looked like it would hurt, having your belly pinched and squeezed like an elastic band around a half-blown balloon. My, my, my, skinny Zelly had so much to learn about women and sizes! As I look back at photos of me when I started modeling, I went down to 116 lbs. – a size 4 which is today's 0 – at 5 '8, I looked skeletal which is exactly what my then husband, Jack said to me. I scoffed at what he said, since the prevailing sentiment was you can never be too thin or too rich.

I am appalled and astounded by my ignorance back then. I was obsessed over NOTHING. Nowadays I am up two shoe sizes and two ring sizes, now that is cause for concern.

I was jolted back to the present at the sound of the captain's voice announcing we were about to land in Puerto Rico. This is the part I wasn't thrilled about. You see I was headed to Carnival in St Thomas, US Virgin Islands, but the airport didn't accommodate jets, so I had to switch to a fifteen-seat plane in PR to get there. I wasn't filled with dread, but I didn't want to make any mistakes either. I certainly didn't want anyone to think I didn't know what I was doing. I clearly understood that wasn't wise, although my mind never actually considered any danger in what I was doing. As I look back at it now, I am blown away that I was allowed to travel alone like that. I marvel that I had the chutzpah to even do it. I remember a friend of mine telling me once, when I was fourteen, having dinner at her house:

"You have a lot of chutzpah!"

"What's that?" I asked.

"It means you say and do just what you want without worrying what can go wrong. You're unafraid, you have nerve. It's a Jewish word we use for people like you."

"Is it a good thing?"

She smiled. "It can be, sometimes yes, sometimes no."

"Hhhmmm," I responded, uncertain whether I'd been complimented or insulted.

The plane hit the ground and bounced a few times before gliding along. Whenever I see a president walking down the steps of Airforce One, I think back to that day. I recall sticking my head out into the blazing heat and blinding sunlight. Adjusting my Sophia Loren movie star sunglasses, my left hand clutched the rail and right hand held tight my mom's coveted Samsonite. I descended the steep stairs and followed along single file, watching those ahead disappear between a fence and a small gray cement building. Inside, I found a bathroom to go in and change to a halter top and a light sweater as it was far too hot for what was appropriate in Jersey. I headed straight to the bathroom sink to splash water on my face, and gasped at what I saw in the mirror! What happened to my sleek, bouncy and behaving hair?! Humidity in New Jersey had nothing on Puerto Rico. My hair went from straight to a curly, frizzy, hot, sweaty mess! Hair pulled back into a ponytail, pale pink tank top on, sunglasses and dangly sparkling enormous fish earrings in place, I was ready for my adventure.

Walking outside to board the "puddle jumper" to St Thomas, I suddenly felt the beginnings of a knot of acid in my belly. Just a little. I actually studied French in school, but I knew enough Spanish to understand what the men were sliding up to me and saying. It was not just *Hi beautiful* or *Hello*. In fact, they were disgusting words meant for the prostitutes in a seedy brothel or words you would reference in *The Story of O* or *Lady Chatterley's Lover*.

The puddle jumper was a sea plane. We came right into the middle of the dock in downtown Charlotte Amalie. It was April and Carnival Time! The air was filled with the sound of steel drums. It was my first time hearing them up close and I loved them. I stepped right off the plane onto the wooden platform and started swinging my hips and dancin to the beat. I giggled, giddy with excitement and joy because the sun was hot on my skin and I was on an island. I threw my head back and laughed enjoying this delicious moment.

I met the guy who was sitting in my mom's kitchen a year later on my second trip.

I learned very early on that everything you think you want is not right for you. To distinguish between a reason, a season and a lifetime.

***

LOVE IN THE MUDD

***

The weekend had started off as usual; sleeping in, chores, and then the dash to the corner of 8th and 22nd to get fresh flowers, a pastrami on rye and a crunchy not too garlicky pickle. I peeked in my favorite antique shop to say *hi* to Mr. Goldstein.

Looking back it was definitely the best of times, and the worst of times to borrow from a famous tome. I closed my eyes and sighed. Lying back on my leopard chaise I adjusted my cat eyed glasses on my nose and looked fondly through hooded eyes at the memory of that night. My lips formed a slightly wicked smile followed by a chuckle out loud.

I loved to curl up at dusk on my favorite leopard lounge, with tea and the latest good read, but today it was a cheap jug of Carlo Rossi Rhine wine and a cheesy romance novel paired with the French chanteuse Edith Piaf. I could have wallpapered an entire room with the fake Fabio paperback covers I had bought in the past year.

Around 9pm I found my way back to the chaise to relax and lose myself in someone else's pathos and erotic going ons.

By midnight, my belly full on peanuts and wine, I dressed in my latest leopard vintage find and headed downtown to the infamous Mudd Club. It was the counterculture of Studio 54 and the coolest spot on earth. Celebs like Andy Warhol, Adam Ant and David Bowie would drop by. People nervously stood in line outside the black velvet ropes (or was it red?) trying to look cool and unbothered while fervently praying the doorman would let them in. I glanced out the corner of my eye at them and strode right up to him and said *hi* with a big smile. I heard the click as he lifted the rope and I was on my way inside, filled with the usual excitement and anticipation of what the evening might bring.

Who would I see and even share a conversation and a line. Part of the charm of The Mudd was that it was small and the kind of place where celebs from art, fashion and music would mingle with regular people hip or beautiful enough to get inside. Who knew back then that even Mudd Club doorman Jean-Michel Basquiat would become an uber-famous artist one day? It was a time of infinite possibilities for all of us, and that night I was headed for the improbability of Love.

Back then I was torn between being quirky and madcapish like Cyndi Lauper, mysterious and sexy like Madonna or cool and edgy like Annie Lennox. This was the '80s and the hardcore feminism of Pat Benetar with her unforgettable anthem *Love is a Battlefield*. I was even lured in by the music of the manic and rebellious Miss Wendy O Williams of The Plasmatics. It was definitely very cool to be a girl during that era, and song titles were a further indication of just how powerful and popular we were. There was Cyndi's *Girls Just Want To Have Fun*, Madonna's *Material Girl* and Annie's *Who's that Girl.* As for me, I believe I had a little piece of each of those women inside me, except the manic part – I was fairly well balanced and never self-destructive.

I lived for that music and I danced wildly around my tiny one room studio apartment in Chelsea, singing the tunes of Bananarama, Go Go's, Bangles, The Pointer Sisters and my favorite boy band The Specials. My holiday favorite song *Christmas Wrapping* was from a lesser-known group, The Waitresses, and their hit song *I Know What Boys Like* was my own secret anthem. Such a shame the lead singer died so young. I still play *Christmas Wrapping* at the start of each holiday season.

Yes, it was an extraordinary time for women. They were celebrated for being creative, and appreciated for being independent and empowered. I, for one, had never felt freer and more excited to be alive. I had a dream job I truly loved as a casting agent in my dream city NYC. I was making decent money and I greatly enjoyed all the perks of being in the industry, especially the gallery openings and The Emmy parties. Besides, every day was a fresh, exciting new challenge.

It was payday and I sashayed my little tits and buns into the Norma Kamali store to purchase the most exquisite piece of clothing I have ever owned – then or now. I'd been jealous of the mannequin as I stared at her in the window every day for a month.

"I know, I know." The salesgirl laughed as I turned and pointed to the window. She helped me ease my arms into the most fabulous Russian Cossack style coat like on the set of a movie. It had silky black faux fur on the inside, on the massive cuffs and collar, and beautiful sleek leopard faux fur on the outside. It was the most expensive coat I had ever owned at $2,750. *PLUS* that freakin NYC tax. It was almost six months' rent! But it was a must have, besides I knew all the best thrift shops and how to mix them with bargains at Bloomies and designers showroom sales to give the appearance of wealth, which was the ultimate goal. There was just one little drawback to my immense pleasure and pride in my new Kamali Cossack Coat, it literally weighed nearly thirty pounds! When you consider that it was 20% of my weight, that was one heavy load to carry, but you know I did it. I strutted right out the door, bundled up in my Kamali coat, Betsy Johnson crinoline and Doc

Martens,feeling like a Hollywood movie star or at least like an Off Broadway star.

That night tying up my Doc Martens I looked longingly at the coat, but no way.

Once safely inside the velvet ropes, I stopped by the bar and, seeing no one interesting, hot or famous to chat with, I made my way to the dance floor. I was in the middle of the floor, one arm waving wildly, hips thrusting to the beat of The Specials' song *Gangsters*. Suddenly a guy appeared in front of me smiling, flailing his arms and gyrating; mimicking, yet slightly out of sync with my movements.

"Whoops!" he shouted, and the vodka tonic glued to my right hand was all over my lower half.

"Golly!" he said, then disappeared.

"Let me." He was down on his knees in front of me attempting to wipe the liquid dripping down my legs.

"Stop! What are you doing?!" I said, embarrassed that a stranger was down on the floor exuberantly scrubbing and touching my legs, albeit with good intentions.

He looked up at me with such pure innocence and something else, making my heart skip a beat. Just a little barely noticeable beat skip.

He rose and together we moved through the sea of bodies off the dance floor.

I could feel the cold cement of the wall against my sweating back as he leaned in, his eyes locked intensely on mine. I could hear my own breathing and my mind barely registered the fact he was going to kiss me, as my eyes closed and his warm lips met mine too briefly. He fully leaned against me, wrapping his arms around me, and pulling me in close he nestled his face in my neck. We clung to one another for what seemed an eternity, just breathing and breathing in one another as if we could not get enough.. I could feel in his kiss a hunger for a connection, not exactly passion and sex, although it was so passionate it literally took my breath. It was more than the *I want to screw you* kind of passion, so I was unafraid,yet very much afraid.

That first look, the kiss, the hug were shocking, puzzling and fascinating to me and I wanted to know more. Gently untangling, and pushing him away so we were no longer touching, I leaned my head back so that I could fully see his face.

"What's your name, Mister I-spill-drinks-on-and-a kiss-a stranger?"

"I'm sorry... so sorry... didn't mean to do that... spill the drink... and the kiss. I'll pay the cleaning bill..." He was so cute as he rambled and stuttered, expressing his dismay and concern. He stopped and looked at me for help, arms dangling at his side.

Breaking my own personal code for the second time. I slid my arms around his neck, hands tangling in his hair. I pulled his head down and kissed him so hard that a moan escaped from deep inside him or was it me. It just seemed the next thing to do.

"My name is Gene Wadsworth Longfellow. I drive a cab at night and go to auditions during the day. I left Ohio to become an actor."

He had a strange ethereal quality to his voice, and I listened, mesmerized. There was a simplicity and purity about him that was so captivating.

I thought about him all day Sunday, berating myself for not giving him my number. I played the experience over and over again in my head. Damn it, damn it, damn it!!! I was restless all damn day and nothing, not even music and my beloved books, brought me peace. Gene Wadsworth Longfellow had stolen my peace of mind. Damn him. Who was he? What if he was the one? Damn me for not taking his number when he offered it to me. His kiss, the way I felt in his arms, his voice haunted me far into the middle of the night.

***

I woke Monday morning sleepy and grumpy, but there was the routine of getting ready for work. I cheered up slightly thinking about the film we were casting that day, and the thought of the audition process and the people I would meet put a smile on my face. As I walked towards the office, I consoled myself with the fact that if Mister Spill a Drink was a contender for Mr Right, he would be back at The Mudd next Saturday night. I thought about what I would say and do. I was deep in thought, examining exactly what I would say.

"Hi, Samantha." This time my heart definitely skipped a beat because he was leaning against the side of the building to my office.

"My name is not Samantha," I said, grinning and walking, almost skipping towards him.

He threw his head back and laughed. I could see his Adam's apple bobbing up and down in his throat.

"Well, what is it?" he asked, gazing at me intently, grinning himself – his head cocked to one side. It struck me again how interesting his voice was, I thought I could listen to it all day.

"How did you get here?" That was a stupid question I thought to myself. "How did you find me?"

"By subway. I asked the bartender at the Mudd Club if he knew you and the casting agency you worked at, so here I am."

"Yes, you are," I said. I stared at him, still stunned to see him there in the daylight. He was as pale as I imagined a bloodless vampire might be.

"Well?" he asked.

"Well, what?" I was distracted by the fact that his amazing hazel eyes hadn't stopped staring into mine. I was still shocked that he was in front of me.

"Your real name?"

"I'm Zelda," I said, putting out my hand.

"Zelda! I love that name," he said, grinning even wider. Ignoring my outstretched hand, he hugged me quickly.

"Zelda, would you go for a hotdog with me?"

That snapped me back to reality.

"No. I would not like to get a hotdog. One, it's 9am in the morning, too early for hotdogs. Two, I'm going to be late for work and, three, I don't do meat in casings except handmade Italian sausages."

He threw his head back and laughed as if I had just said the funniest thing. I laughed as well.

"It's not just any hotdog – it's from Gray's Papaya."

"Anyway, do not think you're going to buy me off with a hotdog just so you can get in good with a casting agent! Mr Want-to-be-an-actor." Why was I talking this way? Mister this and Mister that.

He suddenly looked crestfallen. "I would never do that. I just wanted to see you again and spend some time with you. I didn't mean hotdogs now. I meant later; maybe we could take them to the park. Would you prefer pizza? I know the best pizza joint. I would love to take you somewhere nice on my payday."

I felt bad that I'd accused him, even in jest – kind of in jest – after all, I didn't really know this guy. What I did know was I had to get into work.

"Gene, I have to go in but give me your number and I will call you later."

"Bye!" Snatching the number, I kissed him on the cheek and dashed inside.

***

I arrived home later that evening, I couldn't wait to kick off my shoes and lay back and think about the situation named Gene. Did I really want to get involved with a struggling neurotic actor?

Musicians, artists, actors: my experience with them was they were all a bit neurotic or eccentric. Fascinating people to be around but not for a relationship.

If I had listened to my instincts, I would not have spent two magical years with Gene Wadsworth Longfellow. I would not know what it was like to be worshiped and adored by a person so genuine, thoughtful and caring. His love was so tender it soothed my soul. He kept my heart strings zinging, he was so romantic. He kept me laughing daily with his kooky antics, and his zest for life was matched only by mine. He was like the gentle rain that comes on a hot summer's day that cools the air for a spell.

"Look Zelly! Let's do this, Zelly!" he was always saying to me.

We were like teens discovering love for the first time. We rode on the Carousel and attended concerts in Central Park. We acted out our own imaginary plays at Belvedere Castle during the day, and later we walked with his arm tight around my waist to see a real play at Shakespeare in the Park.

In my apartment, I rehearsed lines with him for his auditions while he'd lay with his head in my lap. He took me to Gray's Papaya and he had the famous hotdog and I had the Papaya King drink. Sitting on a bench as we chatted and dreamed, and made plans for the future. We went boating in Central Park while he serenaded me with old love songs. We danced many nights away at the place that brought us together, the Mudd Club, and wrapping his arms around me we'd kiss as if we were all alone. We spent time eating and playing Monopoly and cards with my friends and family in

Jersey. We even took the long drive out to Youngstown, Ohio, because he wanted to introduce me to his family.

After a seven-hour drive across the Pennsylvania turnpike we were parched and hungry. His mother immediately took me into the kitchen and confided in that gentle sweet voice of hers:

"I'm frying chicken for the first time. Am I doing something wrong?"

I looked at the pale, limp chicken in bubbling butter, crowded together in a broccoli steamer and replied:

"My mom always fries chicken in oil in the frying pan, but no worries because I can't fry chicken myself."

As we laughed, she said:

"Tuna sandwiches coming right up!"

At the table, listening to his parents talk, I took a big swig of lemonade and immediately it projected out my mouth across the table landing in his father's plate.

Mortified and embarrassed, I clasped my mouth and gasped. Staring at the tiny lump of tuna on his father's plate, all eyes shifted to me as I stuttered "I am so, so sorry but I despise gin!"

That dear sweet, cute as a button Mrs. Longfellow had put a huge amount of gin in that lemonade and sheepishly admitted that the glass was intended for her. No one I knew put alcohol in lemonade back then. Nor would they serve it unannounced with tuna. She later confided to me it was to keep her hot flashes in check. She said she had hot flashes that would sometimes cause her to go outside naked in the snow. I smiled and listened to her with raised eyebrows, nodding my head from time to time. I prayed I would never have hot flashes like Mrs Longfellow.

And so our time together was filled with making wonderful, loving memories. We each gave it everything we had in us to give, but sometimes even everything is not enough. We were still in love but we both knew that after nearly two beautiful, mostly happy years our season together was coming to an end. He had to let me go.

I made the decision to leave the city. It was just too painful to be in Manhattan with all its memories of our love. I decided to start a new career and move to the Islands. It was heartbreaking for both of us. At the airport he wrapped his arms around me one final time, pulling me so close I could barely breathe.

He whispered in my ear, "Zelly I love you. I will always always love you my Zelda," and nestled his face in my neck one final time.

There's something about a man who nestles his face in your neck that says he's so vulnerable it clutches my very soul. We clung to one another and cried for what we were and couldn't be, what we had and couldn't have.

So, dear reader, I headed for a new life in the Virgin Islands and left behind Gene Wadsworth Longfellow, who sadly – in spite of our great love and all of our efforts to change the situation – was still a virgin.

As I boarded the plane, turning to wave one final time, I saw him standing there staring at me with those intense eyes. He already looked so alone. Tears streamed down my face; I could barely breathe. My throat was closing up. I swallowed hard trying not to sob out loud.

Natalie Cole's song popped in my head.

"I miss you like crazy, I miss you, baby
A love like ours will never end
Just touch me and we're there again."

***

Mrs Yogi Berra's Modified Chicken Recipe

ZELLY'S
MODIFIED TUMMY CONSCIOUS
secret
RECIPES

In memory of my experience at Yogi Berra's house. I asked Mrs Berra for the recipe which I have modified over the years. This simple recipe has replaced my Christmas turkey. I call it home run chicken for two obvious reasons

Mrs B's Home Run Chicken

6 boneless chicken breasts
2 ribs of celery diced chunky
1/2 of medium yellow onion diced (optional)
Pepperidge Farm Classic bread stuffing 12 oz bag
Adobo seasoning or what you prefer
S&P
Butter unsalted 5T, Olive oil

Pound chicken breasts flat
Sprinkle a bit of salt and pepper on the inside
Adobe on the outside
Put 1T butter in a sauté pan with diced onions and celery cook until lightly wilted
Substitute water and pour in pan add 3T butter boil
Add stuffing mix last and stir until mixed (don't overdo)
Add stuffing to breast and secure with toothpicks
Bake seam side down foil covered for 10 minutes on 400
Melt 1t butter and 2T olive oil together
Uncover and pour mixture over chicken breasts
Continue to cook uncovered for about 30-40 minutes
If overcooked serve with chicken gravy or Knorr hollandais sauce :)
Optional-put in walnuts, dried cranberries,apples.sausage

***

NOTES

Letter from the Author

Dear New and Old Friends,

I sincerely hope you enjoyed my first book. I have three stories already written for my second book. If you enjoyed this book, you could support me in a number of ways.

1. Ask your local bookstore to order it.

2. Write a review on Amazon, Barnes and Noble, etc.

3. Ask for it on Goodreads or any other site.

4. Suggest it for your book club.

5. Gift it or suggest it to friend.

Thank you so much in advance for supporting me and Zelly (wink wink)

Hugs and Love, Ramona

This book is the first book in the series of Zelda's Secrets. Next up Zelda's Secrets Part 2

PUBLISHERS NOTE

Go to KISMET Publishers books for Conversation Starters.

www.kismetpublishers.com

www.ingramcontent.com/pod-product-compliance
Lightning Source LLC
Chambersburg PA
CBHW061219210726
48294CB00006B/1900

* 9 7 8 1 7 3 9 3 8 7 0 5 1 *